sew with sara

PJs, Pillows, Bags & More
Fun Stuff to Keep, Give, SELL!

Sara Trail

C&T PUBLISHING

Publisher: Amy Marson

Creative Director: Gailen Runge

Acquisitions Editor: Jan Grigsby

Editors: Jake Finch, Kesel Wilson, and Stacy Chamness

Technical Editors: Nanette S. Zeller and Rebekah Genz

Copyeditor/Proofreader: Wordfirm Inc.

Cover/Book Designer: Kristy K. Zacharias

Production Coordinator: Zinnia Heinzmann

Illustrator: Tim Manibusan

Photography by Christina Carty-Francis and Diane Pedersen of C&T Publishing, Inc., unless otherwise noted

Published by C&T Publishing, Inc., P.O. Box 1456, Lafayette, CA 94549

Library of Congress Cataloging-in-Publication Data

Trail, Sara,

Sew with Sara : PJs, pillows, bags & more : fun stuff to keep, give, sell! / Sara Trail.

p. cm.

Summary: "Thirteen-year-old Sara teaches teens and 'tweens to sew and how to make money selling the items they make. Nine projects included"--Provided by publisher.

ISBN 978-1-57120-603-9 (paper trade : alk. paper)

1. Sewing--Juvenile literature. I. Title.

TT712.T73 2009

646.2'1--dc22

2008041963

Printed in China

10 9 8 7 6 5 4 3 2 1

Dedication

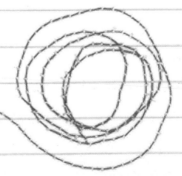

To my aunt Emory, who could have been my mom: "…I make my mom dresses and things while your boy leaves you bathtub rings!" You've got a Funky Son!

Love,

Your Sister's Daughter (Sew Sara)

contents

Acknowledgments

I want to acknowledge and especially thank all the following people:

My mom and dad, Eddie and Katrinka Trail: Thanks for all the time, encouragement, and expensive trips to the fabric stores!

Grandma Emma: I love and miss you. You taught me to stop wasting scrap material and proclaimed me "the most busy, energetic, non-sleeping, creative grandchild" you have ever loved to babysit!

Grandma Missouri Trail: You just loved the safari-themed quilt I sent you for your bed in Toledo, Ohio. If your friends want to place orders, just have them call Eddie (your son and my dad)!

Grandpa Tate: I know you don't know much about sewing because you can only do work as a lawyer. I am glad you think my work is pretty, and I will consider law school—don't worry!

Great-Aunt Mal: Thank you for your early instruction. Your patience and kindness were extraordinary. I can't imagine letting a five-year-old into my sewing closet with scissors the way you did! I hope one day to have enough money to repay you for all the cut-up, discarded fabric I left behind!

Mr. Dan Schoenberg, owner of The Sewing Machine Shop in Walnut Creek, California: Thank you for your incredible kindness and interest in my development. Please consider me for a job when I am old enough to get a work permit. I promise to work really hard and not talk too much!

My neighbor, Shelley Bowen: Thank you for your many evenings of instruction and encouragement and great home-baked treats.

Mrs. Bernie of Queen B's Quilt Shop: Thank you for letting me take your adult quilting classes! Mom said they were cheaper than hiring a sitter for me. ☺

I know that sometimes I talked a lot and made a nuisance of myself, but remember that I'm getting older by the day, and I'll try to keep my mouth closed more and my ears open more, too!

Miss Eleanor: How can I thank you enough for your expert training? Thanks for answering my constant phone calls. Thanks for letting me use your PayPal account and teaching me how to order fabulous fabric via the Internet. Thank you for taking me to all the trade shows and advanced classes. Thank you for letting me use your brand-new Bernina sewing machine.

My two grandmas live far away, one in Alabama and the other in Ohio, and it seems that you found me when I needed you most. I love you and will never forget the dreams you have helped me reach. You are so patient and kind, and I love sewing with you every week. Even if I get famous, I'll never stop wanting to come over to your sewing studio to sew with you until you get tired!

Miss Jan Grigsby: Thank you for coming to my house so many times to check in on me and my step outs. I think I understand better now how to be focused.

introduction

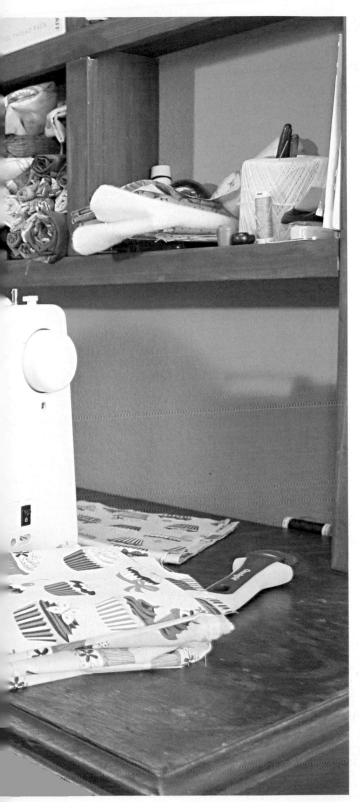

Sew Sara!

Hey! My name is Sara (no "h" here!!!). I am a new book author, and I am thirteen years old. Actually, when I started writing this book, I was twelve years old. **No doubt you are wondering, "How did a kid like you get a chance to write a book?"** Good question! First of all, let me say that it was a blessing from God because He placed a lot of wonderful people in my life.

When I was four years old, my mom loved to sew quilts. I would beg my mom to let me help her sew on her sewing machine. (My grandma said that my mom was a new mom and was really taking big risks to let me sew because I might end up in the hospital emergency room!) My mom would let me sit on her lap and help guide the fabric under the sewing machine needle while she sewed quilts. She said that because of my help, it would take her three times as long to complete any quilting projects, but it was worth it because she knew how much I loved to sew. Mom also said that she warned me to keep my fingers back from the needle, but she knew that if my fingers got pierced, it wasn't my heart, brain, liver, or lungs!

When I was younger, we lived in Merrillville, Indiana, and my great-aunt Malarie was my second sewing teacher. While my mom was at work, I would go to my aunt's house and sew on her sewing machine. I was five years old. Great-Aunt Malarie predicted to my mom that I would probably never slow down long enough to be a careful seamstress because I was always starting a project and rushing through it, unwilling to pick out any of the mistakes or sloppy stitches I made.

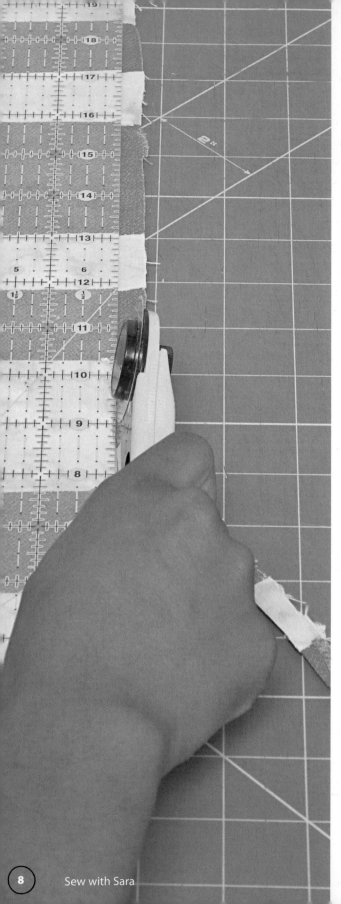

My third teacher was my neighbor, Shelley, who lived three doors down from my current home in Antioch, California. **I was eight when Shelley, a kind mother of four boys, introduced me to rotary cutting by buying me a rotary blade and cutting mat for Christmas.** She taught me how to quilt in the evenings when her small boys were asleep. I can remember coming home with strip sets for a quilt and having my mom ask me what in the world I was doing, because my mom used only scissors and very basic quilting techniques.

After learning all I could from the adults around me, I begged my father to take me to downtown Antioch, where a local quilting fabric shop offered adult classes. I was nine when my father walked me into the shop, Queen B's Quilt Shop, and I met the owner, Mrs. Bernie. Things really took off then. Mrs. Bernie allowed me to enroll in many of the adult classes, and then I began to advance because of all the wonderful ladies who helped me along the way, especially Mrs. Sally. From then on, I started teaching my mother advanced quilting techniques.

My mom set up a small area in her office for me to sew while she worked. In my mother's office, I began making wonderful quilts and pillows. I would show them to my friends at school and church. Many of the girls at my church were very interested in learning how to sew, and our pastor, Henry Kelly, decided he would start a ministry called "The Grace Temple Sewing Studio." Pastor Kelly bought eight inexpensive sewing machines. It was then that the most influential teacher of my life walked into the sewing studio and volunteered to help teach all of us girls and boys how to quilt.

My current teacher and mentor is Miss Eleanor O'Donnell. Miss Eleanor and I spent many hours together teaching all the kids who were interested in sewing. I consider Miss Eleanor my third grandma, and she allows me to spend twenty hours each week sewing at a level I could never have imagined. Miss Eleanor and I still spend quite a bit of time each week in her sewing studio, sewing quilts and other things. Because of her kindness and love, I have learned many advanced techniques that would have taken me years to learn while sewing on my own!

Well, that brings me up to the present. **Here I am, writing this book, hoping that I can share my love for sewing with all the kids in the world who enjoy creating like I do.** My mom asked the C&T Publishing acquisitions editor, Jan Grigsby, to come to our house and help me stay focused on getting all the projects done for my book. Miss Jan is a very nice lady, and she is the one who I originally met and asked if I could write a teenage book for C&T Publishing. Now that Miss Jan has come to my house to help, she has seen the real me. I hope she still thinks I am really sweet and nice even though she had to talk to me a couple of times. I went to sleep in the afternoon one time when we were in the middle of getting everything finished up because I was tired. I think that Miss Jan did not like that, but I felt better in the morning and did finally get it accomplished. Let me say that writing a book is a lot of hard work, and it certainly was not as easy as I thought it would be!

Never Be Stressed!
Make Something New and Get Dressed!

Dear Journal,

This is the greatest day of my life! Today I begin 2 write down my ideas and actually write a book about my favorite topic—sewing! I wonder what the other kids my age will think about what I write? I hope they like what I do & I will give it my best!

Signed,

Unstressedly Yours—Sara

About the Author

I live near Oakland, California, with my mom, dad, and two dogs. Right now, I'm in ninth grade. I love sewing, reading, swimming, go-carting, and making money! My family and I attend Grace Temple Church of God in Christ, where I work with other kids in a church-based sewing program. I have many friends and love to have pool parties at my house. I also love to babysit and sew clothes for little girls, and maybe I'll be a fabric and fashion designer.

When I was in fourth grade, I was reprimanded for being a young entrepreneur by my principal! Once a week, my mom would bring me a fast-food lunch. I sold my French fries to my friends for a quarter apiece. I was making as much as $5 in quarters weekly, unbeknownst to my parents! But I don't do that anymore.

I play the piano and have performed "Think of Me" from *The Phantom of the Opera*. I get really nervous when I play for large crowds, but it's fun to give a good performance!

School is okay but homework is not. If only I could just go to school and never have homework! But I do it. I can hardly wait to grow up, go to college, and have my own dorm room so I can keep it messy if I want!

Sew with Sara

I love thrift stores where I can buy old, gaudy clothing and remove the beautiful embellishments, beads, and trims with a seam ripper. Then I put them on thrift store jeans and jackets. I don't spend my allowance on designer shoes and dresses because it's more fun to make my own designer-looking clothes! I buy junky jewelry for a few dollars and add it to the handbags and tote bags I make. Helping my mom re-cover furniture from thrift stores to make it look better is also cool!

I love to stay up late at night and sew. My mom and dad sometimes turn off the circuit breaker in my sewing room so I can't get up in the middle of the night and sew until 3 a.m.! I know I need my sleep for school, but sometimes the desire to finish a quilt can make me crazy!

Please visit me at my website, www.sewsarasew.com!

Halloween? U Be the Costume Queen!

Dear Journal,

At my school we call October 31st Hallelujah Night. When I was chosen to be Glinda the Good for the Wizard of Oz play, I made a beautiful pink costume complete w/ a wand and hat. I will have to wear that costume cuz Mom said that she will not buy new fabric for a new costume when I have a perfectly good one 2 use. I would rather be a "motorcycle mama" but I don't want 2 spend all my money buying all the expensive black leather & stuff...Mom said that if I really wanted 2 make a new costume, I would spend my own money, so I am Glinda the Good...again!

Signed,

Almost Harley-Davidson Sara

tools

In order to make the projects that are in my book, you will need most of the tools I have listed below. If this is your first time sewing, **please don't think you have to buy expensive tools and fancy fabrics and stuff.** Instead, check with family and friends and see if they know someone who sews. They may have extra tools or fabric they can give you. If not, look for sales and buy budget-type supplies and fabric. When you have more experience sewing, you might want to buy higher-quality supplies and give your old tools to someone just starting.

When I started really sewing on my own, I gathered a lot of my basic tools from the dollar store, and my relatives had plenty of unused fabric stored in their closets that they were happy to give me. **Most of the projects in this book can be made from leftover scrap fabric,** so don't think you have to buy everything new. Remember that for beginners, any decent working sewing machine will do! Many adults have unused sewing machines around their homes. Ask and someone might let you borrow or have theirs. Or have your mom take you to yard sales. Sometimes you can find a good, used sewing machine cheap.

The "Must Have" Supplies

Here is a list of the basic sewing supplies you'll need for the projects in this book. Most of the supplies can be found at your local fabric store or the fabric section of your local discount store. You might already have many of the items around your house.

○ **Fabric:** I use good-quality 100% cotton quilting fabric. It comes in lots of pretty colors and styles, it is easy to sew with, and it washes well. Avoid anything synthetic, because it might melt when you iron it. Read Directional Fabric, page 29, before cutting your fabric.

Ouch! I Mean, Really, Ouch!!

Dear Journal,

Bad news! Today I was sewing on a quilt block & Mom's cell phone rang so instead of stopping the sewing machine, I answered the phone & pushed my pointer finger under the needle! The needle went into my finger & it really hurt. I didn't cry & I hated 2 tell Mom about what I had done. Mom always warns me 2 B careful on the machine & for now, I'm going 2 start listening! It's lucky that I did not have 2 go 2 the hospital & get stitches.

omg,

Living and Learning, Sara

○ **Sewing thread:** A basic 100% cotton (or cotton-covered polyester) all-purpose sewing thread will work best for the projects in this book. Avoid embroidery and decorative threads because they are tricky to sew with and won't wear as well. Don't use hand-quilting thread because the coating on the thread will damage your sewing machine.

○ **Sewing machine:** Use a machine that makes straight and zigzag stitches, that is in good working condition, and that you know how to operate. Read Sewing Machines, pages 20–24, before using your machine.

○ **Iron with steam and ironing board or pad:** Almost any brand of iron will do. I think a steam iron works best. Read Ironing, page 25, before using an iron.

○ **Fabric scissors:** Make sure they're good-quality scissors and you use them to cut *only* fabric and thread—*nothing* else. Consider labeling them to warn trespassers against using them without your permission.

○ **Paper scissors:** Any inexpensive scissors will work fine for cutting paper. Just don't use them for cutting fabric; it could be difficult.

○ **Rotary cutter:** Rotary cutters look like fancy pizza cutters. They are very helpful in sewing, but you can use fabric scissors for most of the projects in this book. You can buy a rotary cutter in a kit that includes a mat and ruler. Use a cutter with a safety button that "locks" the blade so you can avoid accidentally cutting yourself. Rotary cutters can be very dangerous! Read Rotary Cutters, Mats and Rulers, pages 26–27, before buying or using a rotary cutter.

○ **Rotary ruler:** I recommend using a 6″ × 24″ ruler. If you buy a kit, this ruler is usually included. If the kit doesn't have the 6″ × 24″ size, you might consider getting one at some point because this size comes in handy for many uses.

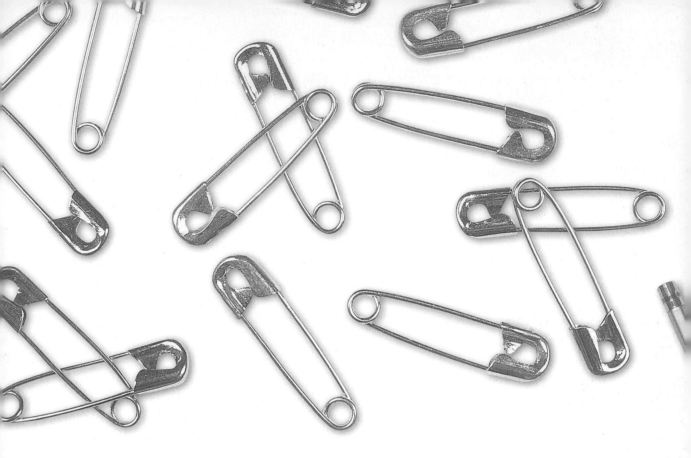

○ **Rotary mat:** This plastic cutting mat has grid marks and is specifically designed for using with a rotary cutter. Buying a kit that has the rotary cutter, mat, and ruler is usually a pretty good bargain. Read Rotary Cutters, Mats, and Rulers pages 26–27, before using rotary tools.

○ **Sewing machine needles:** There are many sizes and styles of sewing machine needles. For the projects in this book, a universal needle, size 70 or 80, will work fine. If you ever do fancier sewing, you'll need to learn more about the different needles.

○ **Hand-sewing needles:** You'll use lots of sizes, so look for variety packs.

○ **Safety pins:** You'll find many uses for safety pins, so look for variety packs of different sizes.

○ **Straight pins:** Look for the kind with colorful glass heads. They're easier to use and won't melt if you iron over them.

○ **Seam ripper:** You *will* need this to help "unsew" your mistakes.

○ **Cloth measuring tape:** You need this for making clothes and measuring large pieces of fabric.

○ **12˝ school ruler:** You will use this for marking lines for cutting.

○ **Yardstick:** You will use this long ruler for drawing long lines.

- **Chalk dressmaker's pencil:** You will want a pencil or pen that will wash out of fabric when dabbed with water. I use chalk, but there are more expensive pens that have disappearing or water-soluble ink.

- **Calculator:** A basic (add and subtract) calculator will work. Yes, sewing requires using your math skills!

- **Pencil or chopstick:** You will use this tool for making neat points when you push out the corners of fabrics.

- **Fusible interfacing or batting:** These materials are usually sandwiched between layers of fabric to give extra sturdiness to projects like tote bags. Fusible materials mean they have a layer of heat-activated adhesive (glue). When you iron them, they become glued to the surface.

- **Parchment paper:** This cooking paper is available in most grocery stores where you find wax paper and plastic wrap. Sewers use it to protect their ironing surfaces from sticky glue when they use fusible materials (see School Folder, page 97).

- **Heavy paper or card stock:** You will use this paper to make heavy patterns (or templates) that can be traced (see Child's Apron, page 54). Card stock can be found in the paper section of an office supply store or the scrapbooking section of a craft store.

- **Appliqué pressing sheet:** (Optional) This non-stick sheet can be used instead of parchment paper to protect your ironing surface from sticky messes. Parchment paper is a much cheaper option.

- **Spray starch:** You will use spray starch when you iron many fabrics. It helps make the fabric easier to sew.

Accidents Happen—Again!

Dear Journal,

I go 2 the church 2 teach other children how 2 sew quilts. Usually it is a lot of fun, but last night there was a new girl who had just learned how 2 oper8 the sewing machine. Well, the sewing machines R all on tables & we all sit pretty close together. The new girl made a mistake & pressed the foot pedal belonging 2 another student's machine. It was a disaster! The other student, a boy, hollered out in pain because his machine sewed the side of his finger! The poor new girl felt so sorry & terrible for her mistake & the boy was yelping in pain. Moral of the story: I must keep everyone seated very far from each other so that no 1 gets hurt like that again. My mom said it was her fault & she will bring in some extra chairs & warn everyone about this problem from now on.

Sew Sara

the basics

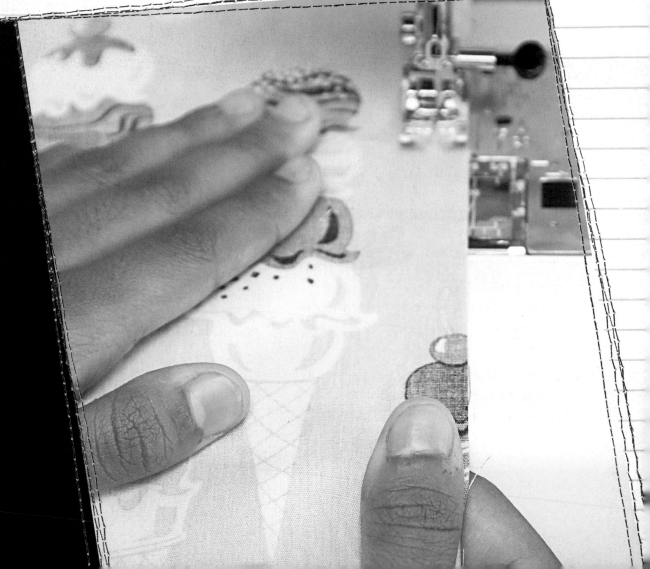

Sewing Vocabulary

○ **Backstitch:** Used to secure stitches when sewing. Stitch a couple of stitches forward, reverse the stitching for a couple of stitches, and resume stitching forward.

○ **Basting stitch:** Used to temporarily hold layers of fabric together. The basting stitch uses long stitches made by hand or by machine.

○ **Bodice:** The upper part of a dress or top that covers a woman's chest.

○ **Casing:** A hemmed edge that forms a tube for a drawstring or an elastic waistband.

○ **Fat quarter:** One way quilting fabric is cut and sold. Fat quarters usually measure 18″ x 22″. A quarter-yard of fabric from the bolt is usually 9″ × 44″, so a fat quarter is twice the width and half the length and is a lot easier to use.

○ **Finger-pressing:** Placing pressure on the fabric with your fingers to either open a seam or make a crease.

○ **Hem:** A folded and stitched finished edge of fabric. A hem is usually stitched to make a neat, professional-looking edge on a skirt or pair of pants.

○ **Length of fabric:** The measurement of the fabric as it unfolds off the bolt. When you buy fabric, the yardage measurement is the length of the fabric.

○ **Raw edges:** The cut, unfinished edges of the fabric.

○ **Right (wrong) sides together:** Most fabrics have a right side (the bright, pretty side) and a wrong side (faded or white side). When two pieces of fabric are sewn together, the right (or wrong) sides need to be stacked facing each other, so they match when the seam is complete. The project's instructions will tell you which way to put the fabrics together.

○ **Seam allowance:** In a seam that joins two pieces of fabric together, this is the measurement from the edge of the fabric to the stitching line. I use ¼″ seam allowances for most of the projects in this book. Some sewing machines come with a special foot that helps you sew a ¼″ seam allowance. If you don't have one for your machine, place a piece of masking tape on the throat plate ¼″ to the right of where the needle goes down in the hole.

○ **Selvage:** The tightly woven edges of the fabric. The selvage edge is usually white and printed with information about the manufacturer.

○ **Top stitch:** A straight line sewed on the right side of the fabric. Usually used for a decorative or professional-looking finished edge.

○ **Tulle:** A lightweight, fine netting material used in ballerina tutus and wedding veils.

○ **Width of fabric:** The measurement of the fabric from selvage edge to selvage edge, as it comes off the bolt. The width of quilting cotton fabric is usually 40″–44″.

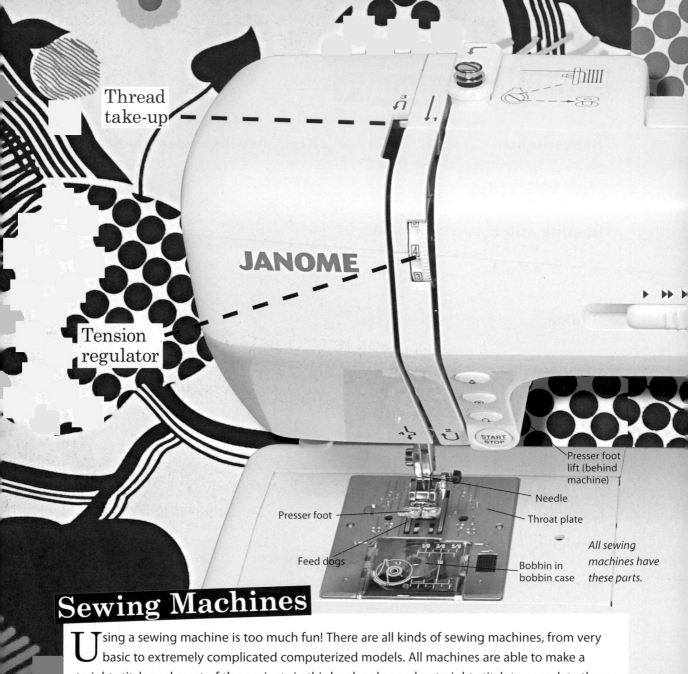

Thread take-up

Tension regulator

Presser foot lift (behind machine)

Needle

Presser foot

Throat plate

Feed dogs

Bobbin in bobbin case

All sewing machines have these parts.

Sewing Machines

Using a sewing machine is too much fun! There are all kinds of sewing machines, from very basic to extremely complicated computerized models. All machines are able to make a straight stitch, and most of the projects in this book only need a straight stitch to complete them.

If you don't know how to work your machine, take it to a sewing machine repair place and ask the technician to check it out for you and show you how to use it. I have found that most of the adults working in sewing machine and fabric shops are really happy to help us young sewers get started! If you don't have a sewing machine manual, ask the technician if he or she can get you one. You also might be able to order one over the Internet if you know the manufacturer and model name (look for a label on the machine). The sewing machine manual is very important for understanding how to use your machine.

Spool pin

Bobbin winder

Flywheel

Stitch width and Stitch length

Decorative stitch option

Power switch

7330

Magnolia

PARTS OF A SEWING MACHINE

For all machines, these are the parts you need to know.

○ **Bobbin:** A small spool under the throat plate that holds thread for the bottom part of a seam. As the thread is wound off the bobbin and picked up by the needle's thread, a two-thread stitch is created by the machine.

○ **Bobbin case:** Holds the bobbin and controls the tension of the bobbin thread.

○ **Bobbin winder:** Holds and spins the bobbin to fill it with thread.

○ **Feed dog:** Moves the fabric under the presser foot as you sew.

○ **Flywheel:** Turns to raise and lower the needle. The flywheel is on the right side of the machine. You can turn it by hand to work the needle very slowly. Or, it will turn fast on its own when you press the foot pedal.

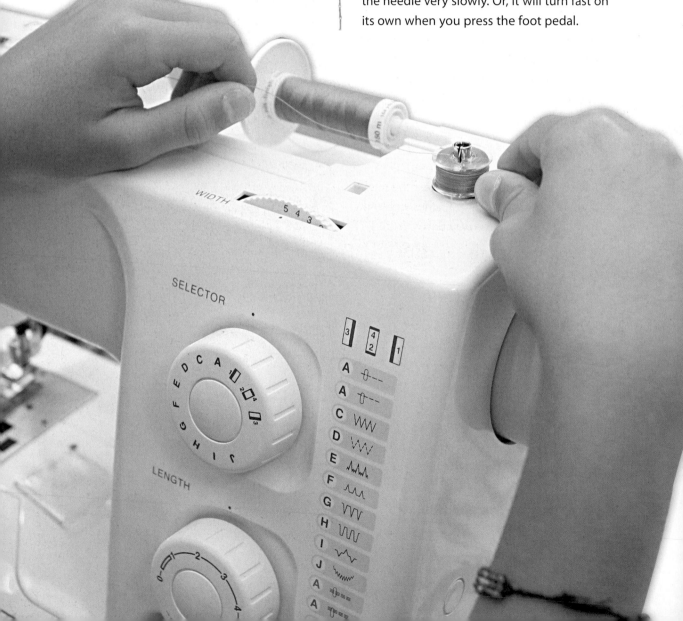

○ **Foot pedal:** Controls the speed of the sewing machine. On most machines, the harder you press the foot, the faster the machine works.

○ **Needle:** Pokes through the fabric at the presser foot. When the needle eye is threaded, the thread is forced through the fabric and grabs and pulls up the bobbin thread to create a stitch.

○ **Power switch:** Turns the machine on and off.

○ **Presser foot:** Holds the fabric in place while you sew. The needle moves up and down through a hole in the presser foot. The foot is raised and lowered with the presser foot lift.

○ **Presser foot lift:** Raises and lowers the presser foot. The presser foot lift is at the back or side of the machine, near the needle and presser foot. Some machines won't sew unless the lift is all the way down.

○ **Spool pin:** Holds the spool of thread while you are sewing.

○ **Stitch length:** Controls the length of the stitch, usually measured by the number of stitches in an inch. Stitch length is adjusted by a knob or lever, or on a computerized machine it's adjusted on the display screen. For the projects in this book, a medium stitch length is fine—not too short and not too long.

○ **Stitch width:** Controls the width of a stitch. It is adjusted by a knob or lever, or on a computerized machine it's adjusted on the display screen. A stitch width of "zero" is a straight stitch. Anything else creates a zigzag or other decorative stitch.

○ **Tension regulator:** Controls the tension on the top thread from the spool. The tension is often tricky to adjust, so if your machine is sewing well don't change the thread tension. If the tension is off, you may get thread "nests" on the back of your stitching or your fabric won't stay stitched together.

○ **Thread take-up:** Holds the thread and helps maintain the thread's tension while you sew. Always make sure when you stop the machine that the take-up arm is at the highest position.

○ **Throat plate:** Covers the feed dogs on the bed (flat surface) of the sewing machine. The throat plate has a hole that the needle goes in and out of.

Sewing Machine Safety Tips

• Always watch where your fingers are! It's very easy to sew your fingers if you're not careful.

• Always move your foot completely off and away from the foot pedal when you're not sewing.

• Sew slowly at first until you get the hang of it.

• If the machine jams, have an adult help you. Never try to fix a jam by yourself!

• Keep track of your bobbin thread.

STARTING TO SEW

Sewing machines are all basically the same. But then, that's like saying all moms are the same. If you're not sure how your machine works, check the manual, ask an adult, or ask the people at the sewing machine repair place.

When you're ready to start sewing, follow these basic steps.

1. Wind a bobbin full of thread.

2. Put the bobbin in the bobbin case.

3. Thread the machine and the needle.

4. Take up the bobbin thread by holding the top thread and turning the flywheel.

5. Put the fabric under the presser foot.

6. Lower the presser foot.

7. Make sure your fingers are out of the way, and gently press the foot pedal to start sewing. The feed dogs will "push" the fabric under the presser foot, away from you, as you sew. The needle will move up and down, creating the stitch.

Sara's Hint

Before you start sewing, take a few stitches on a scrap of fabric from your project. Check the thread's tension and the stitch length and width. If you need to, adjust your machine's settings.

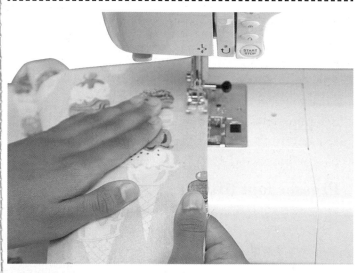

Keep your hands away from the needle when you sew.

TURNING CORNERS

For several of my patterns, you will have to turn corners when you sew the fabric layers together. Here are some simple directions to help you:

1. Use a ¼″ seam allowance to sew along one edge of the fabric layers.

2. Stop sewing ¼″ from the corner, and, using the flywheel, lower the needle into the fabric.

3. Raise the presser foot, and, using the needle as a pivot, turn the fabric to the correct position to sew the next edge.

4. Lower the presser foot, and continue sewing, turning the fabric at each corner.

Ironing

You will need a steam iron for most of these projects. Always iron your fabrics before making a project. It makes things easier if you're working with smooth fabric. A steam iron heats water that you put into the iron and then, with the press of a button, "shoots" the steam onto the fabric. Since I'm using cotton fabric for these projects, irons should be set on "cotton." There are some exceptions, so be sure to follow the directions. The cotton setting is really hot, so make sure you are always aware of where your iron is. It will burn you if you touch it. Always turn the iron off, and unplug it, when you leave the room. This is a good habit to get into, even if your iron has an auto-shutoff feature.

Cutting Pieces with Scissors

All the projects in this book can be made with a pair of fabric scissors. A rotary cutter makes cutting easier, but it takes a lot more skill. To cut pattern pieces with scissors, use an acrylic rotary ruler and chalk pencil to mark the measurements of the pieces on the fabric. Use your fabric scissors to cut out the pieces— straight and slightly to the inside of the drawn lines. Watch what you are cutting, because fabric scissors are sharp!

What Do You Think?

Dear Journal,

I have a friend who is a boy. He is not a boyfriend. (I'm not allowed 2 start dating until I am 16 years old.) Anyway, Desmond is my age & when he comes 2 the church 2 help me sew, he always volunteers 2 press w/ the iron. His dad says he never irons anything @ home. His dad says that he did not know that Desmond even knew how 2 turn on the iron! Desmond has helped me press many quilts & my mom always laughs at this! Do you think Desmond likes me or is he just a really helpful person?

Signed,

Sara-Just-Wondering

Rotary Cutters, Mats, and Rulers

Rotary cutters look like fancy pizza cutters. They make cutting fabric easy, but they are also very dangerous. Ask your parents if they think you're old enough to use a rotary cutter. *Wherever you can, use a good pair of scissors to cut your project materials.*

Use a rotary cutter that has a safety button built into it. The safety button has to be "off" to unlock the blade. Olfa makes several varieties. *Get in the habit of always locking the blade after every cut!* If the blade isn't locked, it's really easy for you or other people to accidentally cut themselves.

A rotary mat is a thin plastic mat that sits on top of a flat surface. All the cutting you do with the rotary cutter needs to be done on a rotary mat! It protects your work surface, and it "grips" the rotary cutter's blade to prevent slipping and really bad accidents.

A rotary ruler is made from clear, heavyweight plastic and is marked with grids and measurements. A rotary ruler allows you to line things up perfectly when you cut with a rotary cutter. Rotary rulers come in a ton of sizes.

Rotary cutters come in several sizes and styles. Use the kind with a safety lock.

ROTARY-CUTTER SAFETY TIPS

Always remember that rotary-cutter blades are very sharp and can really hurt you. For the safest experience, *remember these tips:*

○ Have an adult watch, or help, while you work.

○ Watch where your fingers are at all times. Never put your hands in front of the rotary cutter's path.

○ Cut away from your body, never toward it.

○ Pay attention to what you're doing! Don't watch TV or talk to others while you use the rotary cutter.

○ Cut only one or two layers of fabric at a time.

○ Use a rotary mat on a large, flat surface, such as a table or countertop. Don't cut on the floor; the cutter can easily slip and cut you.

○ Put away your scissors, rotary cutters, and pins after *every* use. You don't want pets or small brothers and sisters to get into them.

○ Have an adult change the blade in your rotary cutter! *Never* change it yourself!

USING A ROTARY CUTTER

If you want to use a rotary cutter, ask your parents for help until *they* feel comfortable with you using one alone. Or, ask them to cut the pieces for you. Here are the steps you should follow to safely and successfully cut your fabric:

1. Place your mat down on a firm, flat work surface, like a dining table or kitchen counter. If you are not tall enough to reach the counter, ask an adult to help you do the cutting. Make sure the entire mat is lying flat on the work surface and that no edges are hanging over.

2. Place your fabric on top of the mat. If the fabric piece is too big, fold it. Press a firm crease in the fabric, which will keep the fabric really flat and allow for a more accurate cut.

3. Line up the folded or straight edge of the fabric along one of the grid lines. These lines are usually spaced 1″ apart.

4. Position the ruler on top of the fabric. Use the ruler's grid lines to line it up with the grid on the mat.

5. Hold the ruler firmly in place and position the cutter along the bottom edge of the ruler. If you're right-handed, the cutter is in your right hand, positioned on the bottom right edge of the ruler, and your left hand is holding down the ruler. If you're left-handed, the cutter is in your left hand, positioned on the bottom left edge of the ruler, and your right hand is holding down the ruler. Hold the cutter with a complete grip. Don't use your index finger to "guide" the cutter forward. The hand holding down the ruler is placed on the ruler and with at least one finger off the (non-cutting) edge of the ruler. Make sure your fingers are not in the way of the rotary cutter.

6. Run the cutter up along the edge of the ruler. Make sure your cut is smooth and the pressure is even from the start to the end of the cut. If you have threads that aren't cut and you know you're pushing firmly, your blade might need to be changed. *Never change it yourself!* Have an adult do it.

Check to make sure your fingers are *not* in the way of the rotary cutter before you begin to cut. My pinkie finger SHOULD be placed off the left edge of the ruler here. Make sure you're safe by securing your finger off the edge.

Using Commercial Patterns

The PJ bottoms in this book (see PJ Bottoms, page 69) can start with a commercial pajama pattern, store-bought PJs, or scrub pants. There are many companies that make sewing patterns for clothes, and almost all of them have patterns for PJs. Commercial patterns are easy to find at fabric stores. Save money and time sewing by shopping for the cheaper easy-to-sew patterns. When you go to the store, be armed with your measurements. For PJ bottoms, you'll need your waist measurement and probably your hip measurement. Don't look for the size you wear in ready-made clothes. Pattern companies don't use the same sizing system; your pattern size will likely be larger than what you wear every day. On the pattern envelope's flap there is usually a chart that will tell you what size pattern and how much fabric you will need to buy based on your measurements.

After you buy the pattern, get it ready by carefully unfolding the tissue-paper pattern sheets. Use an iron on a cool setting, without steam, to press the wrinkles out. The tissue tears easily, so go slowly. On the pattern's instructions, find out what pattern pieces you will need to make the PJ bottoms. Roughly cut out the paper pattern pieces about ½″ away from the outside cutting line.

Prewash your fabric, iron it, and then lay it out on a large flat surface. A floor, without carpet, or a large table will work fine. Place the pattern pieces on top of the fabric, and pin along the inside edges of the pattern. With fabric scissors, carefully cut out the fabric pieces along the pattern's cutting lines. Some patterns have diamond-shaped alignment or registration marks along the edges. Be sure to cut out these marks; they are used to match the pieces together when you sew.

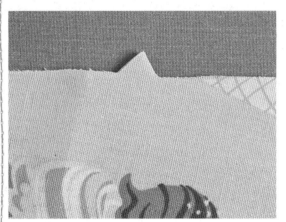

Cut alignment marks into your fabric pieces.

Sew the fabric pieces together, following each step of the pattern's instructions. When I quilt and sew, I normally use a ¼″ seam allowance to join pieces, but most clothing patterns use a ⅝″ seam allowance. Be sure to check the pattern's recommended seam allowance and use it when sewing pieces together.

PJs are a great way to learn how to sew clothes!

Directional Fabric

Quilting cotton fabric comes in a variety of colors and styles. There are some really cute prints in the stores. Many of these prints are directional, meaning that if you turn the fabric one way or another the printed design looks upside down. For example, look at the ice cream cone fabric I used for my PJ bottoms (see PJ Bottoms, page 69). If you are using a fabric with a print that goes only one way, be sure to cut out the pattern pieces so that the print goes the same way on all of them (like, who wants to wear upside-down ice cream cones?).

Fabric direction should be considered for all the patterns, not just the PJs. Pay attention to the direction of the design when you're cutting out the fabric pieces. Or, even better, choose fabrics that don't have a directional design, and you won't have to think about it when you're sewing.

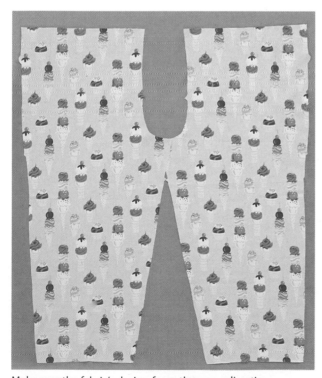

Make sure the fabric's design faces the same direction.

Making Straps

Straps can be used on things like tops, tote bags, or backpacks. The size of the strap depends on what it will be used for. Follow these steps for making straps.

1. Decide how long you want the finished straps to be. Then add at least 2″ to that number to allow enough room for attaching the straps. For example, when I made the Rip-n-Strip Top (page 88) my finished straps measured 12″ long, so I cut them 14″ long (12″ + 2″ = 14″).

2. Decide how wide the finished straps will be. Keep in mind that if your straps are going on a top or dress, the straps need to be wide enough to cover the straps of your bra, if you wear one. Straps for a tote bag or backpack don't need to be as wide. When you know the finished width of the strap, multiply that number by 4 to determine the cutting width. For example, the finished straps for the Rip-n-Strip Top (see Rip-n-Strip Top, page 88) measure 2″ wide, so the cut width for each piece of strap fabric will be 8″ wide (2″ × 4 = 8″).

3. Cut the strap fabric into strips along the **width** of the fabric (see Sewing Vocabulary, page 19). Each strip should measure the width calculated in Step 2.

Sara's Hint

Most quilter's cotton fabric is 42″–44″ wide from selvage edge to selvage edge. You can usually make more than one strap from each strip of fabric. To save time, I cut one long strip of fabric to the width I need, then I follow Steps 4–7 to make one strap about 44″ long. Later, I'll cut this long strap into the shorter lengths I need for my project.

4. On your ironing surface, fold and press the fabric strip in half lengthwise, wrong sides together, to make a center crease.

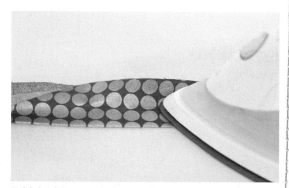

Fold the fabric strip wrong sides together.

Sara's Hint

To iron or not to iron? For some projects, you need a hot iron for things to work well. When making straps, finger-pressing will do just fine. Press on!

5. Open up the fabric strip and lay it flat on your ironing surface. Fold a long edge in toward the center crease, wrong sides together, and press it.

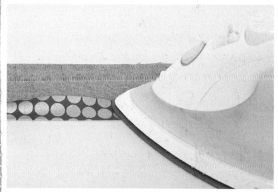

Fold one long edge toward the center crease.

6. Fold the other long edge in toward the center crease, wrong sides together, and press it. You now have 2 folded edges, both meeting at the center crease. It kind of looks like a man's tie from the back!

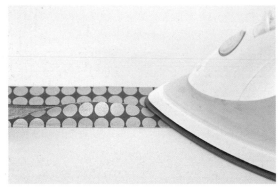

Both long edges are folded in toward the center crease.

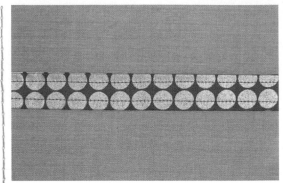

Stitching along both sides makes the straps look professional.

Now let's talk about making some money!

7. Refold and press the fabric strip along the center crease, keeping the raw edges inside this fold. Once the strip is folded, you will *not* see the 2 long cut edges. Topstitch ¼˝ away from the long open edge of the strap. Then topstitch ¼˝ away from the other folded edge of the strap.

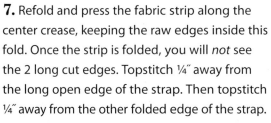

Topstitch ¼˝ away from both long edges.

makin'
money

Iam giving you permission to use the projects in this book to earn money. You can sell the projects to friends and family, or you can host parties where the guests make the projects. When you are comfortable with sewing, you can be a teacher to other kids who want to learn how to sew. Remember that a lot of times your business arrangements are made with the mom rather than the kid, so she is your customer. Before you start trying to sell your projects and services, it's important to understand a few things about doing business.

Ownership

Although I'm giving you permission to use my patterns, most pattern designers don't feel the same way I do. There are laws about copyright ownership, because it is the designer's legal right to decide who can copy, or use, his or her designs. Always get written permission from the designer or publisher *before* you use a pattern to make money. Better yet, do what I do: make up your own design ideas and use those instead of someone else's.

Practice, Practice

It's really important to make the projects at least a couple of times before you try selling them. You need to really know and understand what you're doing. You also need to have good-looking sample projects for your potential customers to see. Practice making the projects so you gain experience and have a variety of samples.

Samples Sell

You can't just show pictures of what you intend to sew. I have a small suitcase to store my samples and other "work" materials in. When a customer is interested in my services, I bring the suitcase so she can see what to expect from my work and pick out what she likes best. Showing the samples really helps sell my work.

Also, you can create a sample book from a spiral notebook or binder. On the pages, glue down 4-inch squares of fabric choices. A customer can use your fabric or buy her own at a fabric store. Tell her how much you'll need for each project. I prefer for the mom to buy the materials so she can pick out what she wants, or I'll go with her and help pick out the fabric. This way I'm not spending a lot of money that I must collect at a later date!

House Parties

After a party, *never leave a mess at a customer's home!* You won't grow your business if you leave messes. Always leave the house cleaner than when you arrived. Most of the guests will be eager to help you clean up after the project is done, so ask for their help. Always ask the mom if everything is in order and clean before you leave her home. Most of your business will come from referrals—one mom telling another mom about you. You probably won't get a good referral if you leave someone's home in a mess.

It's a really good idea—and more fun—to have a friend help with the parties. When a friend helps, you must share the money you've earned! Your friend might even be willing to help you prepare before the party. It is always better to have two experienced people at the party, so all the kids get lots of supervision and you have someone to share the fun with.

On my website, www.sewsarasew.com, I provide tons of ideas about the parties you can host. Some have the guests sewing and others have you sewing the projects beforehand. There are also ideas for handling the business end of what you're doing.

You can make a party out of any of the projects in my book. Just use your imagination! Ask your friends if they would like you to host a sewing party featuring one of the projects in this book. Keep it really simple at first—start out small with a scrunchy or pillow party. As you learn and grow in your sewing business, you will be able to handle more difficult projects!

Keep Promises

With any business, the most important thing is to follow through with your promises. The number one rule is "Don't promise anything you can't do." Another idea is to have backup plans. Let's say you promised to premake aprons for a party and you don't think you'll get them finished in time. *Don't cancel the party or stand your customer up! Instead, come up with a backup plan!* Consider hiring a friend or family member to help you cut fabric or sew.

If you still don't think you'll have things ready on time, contact the mom, explain the situation, and give her other options. Consider offering to use inexpensive store-bought aprons instead of handmade ones. Or consider offering to make a simpler project that you can complete, like a scrunchy or pillow. If you have to change the project, be willing to offer a refund for the difference in cost, but never charge more for your planning errors or other mistakes. You may not make the same money, but you're sure to have fun anyway. Always learn from your mistakes. I sure do!

Earn Cool Ca$h

As a young sewer, you can't expect to make the same amount of money as an adult. A good rule on pricing your work is to never charge more than what you would earn as a babysitter. If you babysit for $4 per hour, then charge only $4 per hour for your sewing time! If you're selling your projects, set your prices to include both the cost of your materials and your time. Remember, people like bargains; if you price things too high, people will not do business with you.

Now go make some cash!

Sara's Hint

You've made enough of these great projects to create a mini store, but where will you sell all of those scrunchies, school folders, and MP3 cases? Everybody who might buy one of your creations is a potential customer. Your job is to price your products reasonably and then to take them to the people who might be interested.

Coming to Terms with Makin' Money!

When a mom comes to you to host a party for her kid, you need to have a very clear agreement between the two of you so there are no problems that come up from misunderstandings. The best way to do this is to put it in writing. Here are most of the things you might have to know or agree on beforehand so that your party can run smoothly.

○ What are the full name, address, phone, and email for your client?

○ What is the date and time of the event?

○ How many people will attend?

○ What are their ages and genders?

○ Where will the party be held?

○ What will you be doing at the party? (Making PJs or painting aprons, for instance.)

○ What special equipment you will need to perform your tasks? (Electrical outlets, tables, or miscellaneous supplies.) And, who is providing the equipment—the host or you?

○ What materials (fabric, glue, paints, for instance) does the host need to provide?

○ What materials will you provide?

○ How much time will you need to do your projects with the guests?

○ Are there any special clean-up supplies you will need?

○ How much will you charge and how? (Per person, by the hour or some other way?)

○ Who will supervise the party?

○ What other items will the host provide? (Food, music, games, etc.)

Short on Cash? Check Your Stash!

Dear Journal,

Being an only child means that my friends R VERY important 2 me. My friend & I have decided 2 start a sewing business 2gether. It's a little scary. We hope that all the moms we know will hire us 2 sew rips & tears & make birthday party favors for their little tots. We also plan on making clothes 4 small dogs from a pattern we bought from the fabric store. We R passing out flyers at school 2 let all the other kids know about our business & some of the girls said they will bring their old blue jeans 2 school so we can take them home & add beautiful decorations like rickrack, rhinestones & trim 2 them. I can't wait 2 see how things go!

Ttyl,

Sara the Entrepreneur

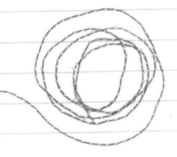

Different places where you can sell your crafts

○ School (Check for any rules that the school might have about this so you don't find yourself in detention!)

○ Church

○ Camp

○ Playgrounds (Sell to the grown-ups, not to the little kids.)

○ Gift shops in your town

○ Flea markets (Try teaming up with a vendor who already has a booth at a market. Maybe you offer to watch her booth for a while in exchange for her having your projects in the booth for sale.)

○ Garage sales (You can host your own or partner with a BFF to hold a sale.)

○ Family and friends (Hey, who else would love helping you out more?)

○ Holiday boutiques (Many towns and organizations hold boutiques near Christmastime to sell homemade products.)

○ Senior centers and homes (Call some in town to find out if they'd let you sell your low-cost goods there. You could even offer free gift wrapping to entice the seniors to buy ready-to-go gifts!)

When you have been doing parties for a while, people will talk about your service and will come to you. Until then, you have to get the word out about your services. There are few things more interesting to grown-ups than a young entrepreneur and that is what you now are. Here are some ways to get the word out about what you're doing.

1. Your local **newspaper** is a natural place to start. Call up the community or business desk and tell the editor about your business. Give it a name. Don't be shy. An email will also work. Editors love to know about kids who are doing things in their town.

2. Another way to get the word out is through **advertising**. You're probably not going to pay for an ad in the paper or on television, but you can post bulletins about what you're selling on community boards. Many are found in libraries, grocery stores, and other places where lots of people come.

3. If you're a tech geek or know of one, you can **create your own website** to promote your stuff. It doesn't have to be complicated, but it must give a way to contact you.

4. Have **business cards** printed up or, even better, picture postcards with your stuff on the front and information to contact you on the back. You should always carry these with you because you never know who might want to buy your projects or hire your party services. (See page 107 for more information.)

5. Hand out fliers at places where moms bring kids, like indoor gyms, dance schools, or playgrounds. (See page 108 for more information.)

6. Talk to **your friends' parents**, especially if your friends have little brothers or sisters.

7. Host an **open house** where people can come and see what you make and what services you offer. Don't do this without your parents' permission!

8. Put a **label** or business card with every item you sell so someone can come back for more!

projects

Cell Phone or
MP3 Player Cover

page 49

School Folder

page 97

Child's Apron

page 54

PJ Bottoms
(for Boys or Girls)

page 69

Envelope
Pillow page 64

Scrunchy

page 75

Tote Bag

page 83

Drawstring Bag

page 78

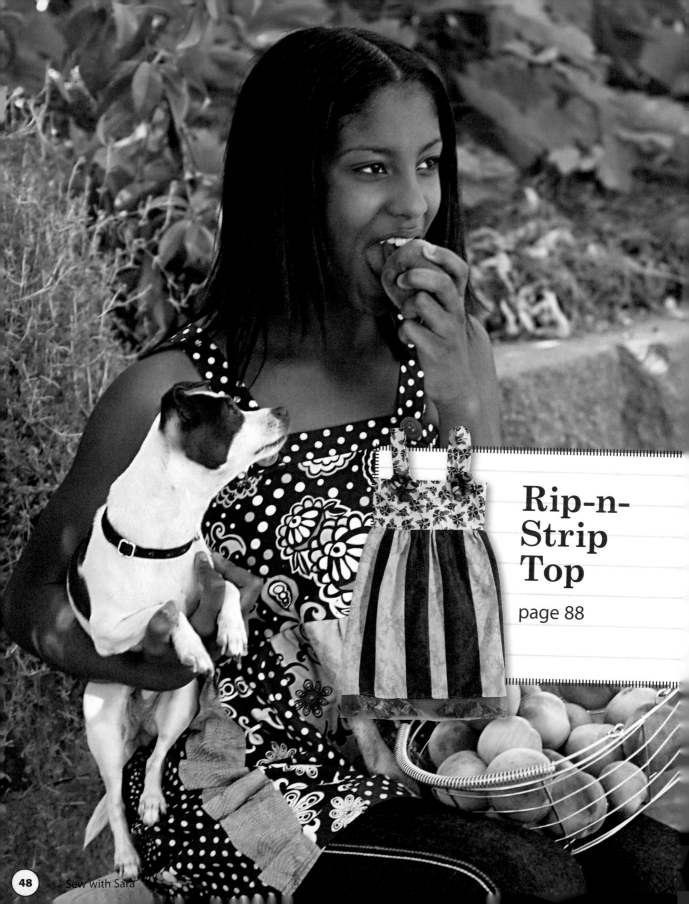

Rip-n-Strip Top

page 88

cell phone or MP3 cover

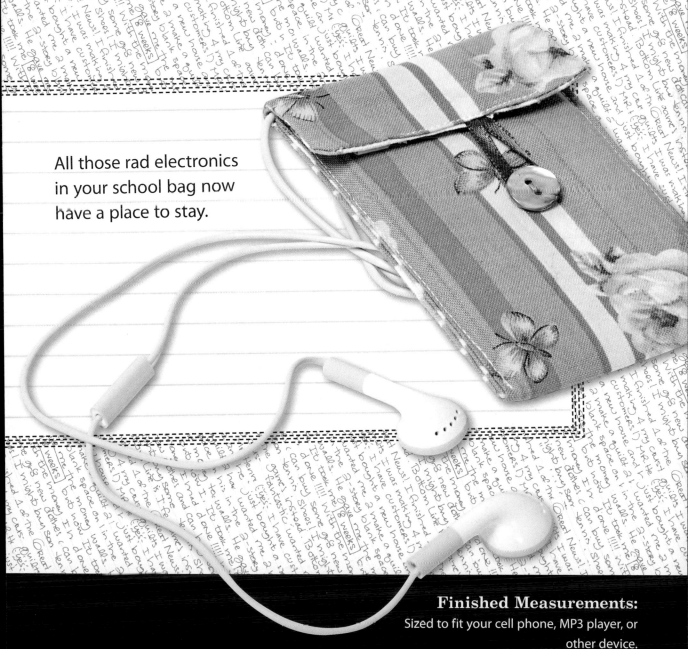

All those rad electronics in your school bag now have a place to stay.

Finished Measurements:
Sized to fit your cell phone, MP3 player, or other device.

Materials

- ○ 2 coordinating fabric scraps
- ○ 4˝ coordinating satin ribbon, ⅛˝ wide
- ○ Button
- ○ Iron-on hook-and-loop tape (optional)
- ○ Matching thread
- ○ Hand-sewing needle
- ○ Pencil or chopstick
- ○ Chalk pencil

Instructions

1. Measure the width and length of the cell phone, MP3 player, or other electronic device, then use the chart to calculate the fabric cutting measurements.

	DEVICE MEASUREMENTS			FABRIC CUTTING MEASUREMENTS
WIDTH		ADD (+) 2˝ =	=	
LENGTH		MULTIPLY BY (x) 2 =	ADD (+) 4˝ =	

2. Use the measurements from the chart to cut 2 rectangles, 1 from each coordinating fabric. Stack them right sides together, edges lined up.

3. Start on a short edge, about 1˝ from the corner. Sew around all 4 sides, using a ¼˝ seam allowance and turning at each corner (see Turning Corners, page 24). Stop sewing about 2˝ from where you started to leave an opening.

4. Trim the corners by cutting them with scissors at an angle. Be careful not to cut through the stitching.

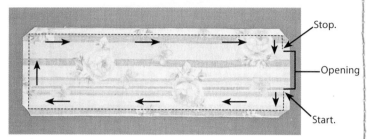

Stitch around the edges, leaving an opening, and then trim the corners.

Sara's Hint

Don't trim too close to the corners, or when you turn the fabric right side out the corners will come apart.

5. Carefully turn the sewn rectangle right side out through the opening, like you would turn a pillowcase inside out. With your fingers, the eraser end of a pencil, or a chopstick, push out the corners, being careful not to push through the stitching.

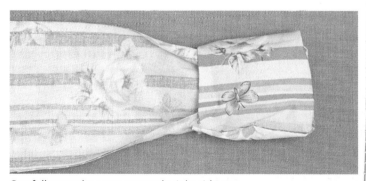

Carefully turn the sewn rectangle right side out.

6. Press the sewn rectangle, making sure the inside seams are pushed out along the edges and are even. Press under the seam allowance at the opening to match the sewn seams.

7. Hand or machine stitch a ribbon loop into the opening.

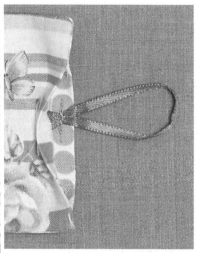

Attach a ribbon loop for a closure.

Sara's Hint

You could also use hook-and-loop tape as a closure. The iron-on kind works great.

8. With the lining sides facing each other, fold the bottom edge of the rectangle up to the top, leaving about 2″ to 3″ for a flap. Topstitch the folded layers together, very close to the edge, to create the pocket.

9. Insert the device, fold the flap over, and mark where you want the button closure to be with chalk. Remove the device, and sew on a button.

Time to listen to some tunes or maybe call a friend!

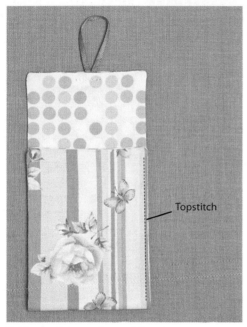

Fold to make a pocket and flap.

Topstitch

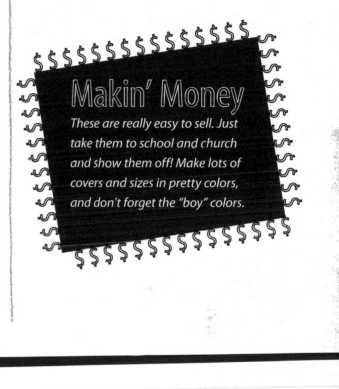

Makin' Money

These are really easy to sell. Just take them to school and church and show them off! Make lots of covers and sizes in pretty colors, and don't forget the "boy" colors.

Piano Drama

Dear Journal,

My piano teacher called my mom 2day & told her that I am not really applying myself & practicing as much as I should. I told Mom that I really don't like piano & I should quit. I have been taking lessons since I was 5 years old. I never really liked practicing but I do love 2 play the piano 4 guests & recitals. My mom said that she does not believe in letting me start something important like music lessons (it was my idea but I was only 5!!) only 2 quit when the going gets tough. I guess I could squeeze some xtra practice btwn riding my go-cart and chatting w/friends. When I have a family, I will tell my kids 2 be careful what they ask 4!

Sara the Beethoven Wannabe

child's apron

For this fun and easy child's apron (think little sister or cousin!), pick your favorite fabrics. You will need four coordinating fabrics. You can easily use large scraps from previous projects or four fat quarters.

Materials

Note: Four fat quarters of coordinating fabric can be used instead of scraps.

- Fabric A, scrap at least 12″ × 12″
- Fabric B, scrap at least 8″ × 12″
- Fabric C, scrap at least 10″ × 18″
- Fabric D, scrap at least 14″ × 20″
- Lining/strap fabric: 1⅛ yards

- Matching thread
- Heavy paper or card stock
- Chalk pencil
- Pencil or chopstick
- Hand towel (optional)

Instructions

1. Cut the fabric into the following sizes:

- **Fabric A:** 1 square, 10½″ × 10½″
- **Fabric B:** 1 rectangle, 6½″ × 10½″
- **Fabric C:** 1 rectangle, 8½″ × 16½″
- **Fabric D:** 1 rectangle, 12½″ × 18½″
- **Lining/strap fabric:**

    1 rectangle, 18½″ × 28½″, for lining

    2 strips, 8″ × width of fabric, for straps

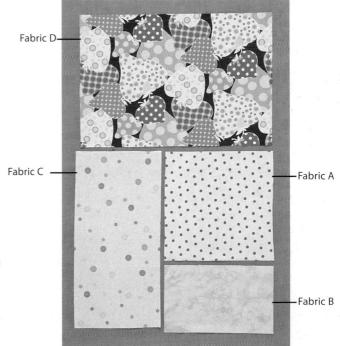

Fabric D

Fabric C

Fabric A

Fabric B

Pieces for the apron front

2. With right sides together, line up and pin the Fabric A square to the Fabric B rectangle along a 10½˝ edge. Sew the pieces together with a ¼˝ seam allowance. Press the seam open.

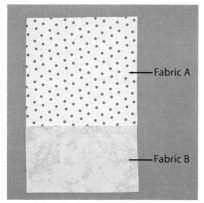

Sew Fabric A to Fabric B.

3. Line up and pin a long edge (16½˝) of the Fabric C rectangle to the section you just sewed, right sides together. Sew the seam, and press it open.

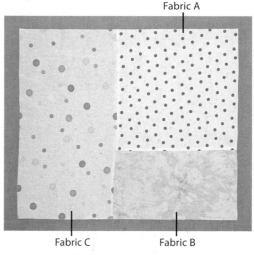

Three pieces are sewn together!

Don't Be Blue. Sew Something Cute & New!

Dear Journal,

It has been raining 4 six days in a row. It's cold & muddy outside & this is the winter for California. You'd think I'd be used 2 it by now. I have a nasty cold & I can't go 2 school or have any friends over. I'm tired of watching television & I don't have any really good books 2 read. Yada yada yada! There is that easy-2-sew pattern I have for aprons. I think I'll get busy! If I make Mom a pretty apron as a surprise, I'll bet she'd be willing 2 take me 4 drive-thru ice cream. P.S.: Sewing machines don't catch colds—they're immune!

Sew Sick Sara

Apron Top

Armhole Template
Child's Apron

Apron Side

cut

4. With right sides together, line up and pin a long edge (18½″) of the Fabric D rectangle to the top of the sewn section, as shown. Sew the seam, and press it open.

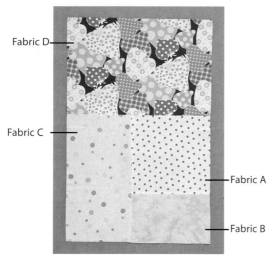

Fabric D

Fabric C

Fabric A

Fabric B

The front of the apron is now sewn together.

5. Place the lining onto the pieced apron front, right sides together. Line up the open edges, and pin them to keep the layers from shifting.

6. Copy or trace the armhole template (page 58) onto heavy paper or card stock. Cut out the template along the solid lines.

7. Line up the armhole template with the top corner (Fabric D rectangle) of the folded fabric. Trace the template's curve onto the fabric with a chalk pencil. Using sharp scissors, cut along the curved line through both layers of the fabric. Unpin.

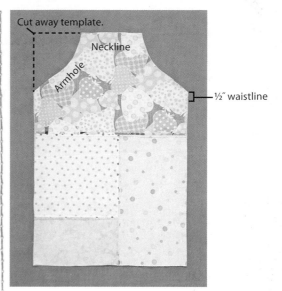

Cut away template.

Neckline

Armhole

½″ waistline

The armholes are now cut from the apron.

Sara's Hint

Sewing Tip: When cutting out the apron's armholes, be sure to cut them small at first and then try the apron on your body. After you see what it looks like, you can cut the holes larger until they are perfect. Don't cut too much the first time. Instead, increase your cuts slowly so that you don't ruin the fabric with a too-large cut!

8. Following the strap instructions (see Making Straps, pages 30–32) make 2 long straps. Cut 1 of the completed straps in half to make 2 waist straps.

9. Lay the pieced apron front, right side up, on your work surface. Working on the right side of the apron, position the neck strap tails on each side of the neckline, about ½˝ in from the armholes, and line up the raw edges at the neckline. Make sure the straps are not twisted, and pin the tails in place.

10. Position each waist strap ½˝ down from the armhole on the right side of the apron at the waistline. Line up the raw edges, and pin in place.

11. Try on the apron, and adjust the strap lengths to fit. I cut my neck strap 22˝ long and each waist strap 20˝ long.

> ## Sara's Hint
> *If the neck strap is too long after you sew it on, just tie a knot in the back of the strap.*

12. Lay the lining on top of the pieced apron front, with the pinned straps in place and right sides together. Line up the edges, and pin the layers together. You now have a sandwich— the lining and pieced front with the straps in between. The straps should not be sticking out; if necessary, tuck the strap tails into the layers, and pin them in place.

13. Start at the middle of the bottom edge and sew around the apron ¼˝ from the edge, turning the fabric at the corners (see Turning Corners, page 24). Make sure you don't sew through the straps except where you want them secured at the waist and neck. Stop sewing about 3˝ from where you started, leaving an opening. Trim the corners by cutting them with scissors at an angle. Be careful not to cut through the stitching.

> ## Sara's Hint
> *If you did catch your straps, don't worry. Simply rip out the few stitches where you caught the strap, move the strap out of the way, and resew.*

14. Turn the apron right side out at the opening. Push out the corners with your finger, the eraser end of a pencil, or a chopstick, being careful not to push through the stitching.

15. Fold under the seam allowance of the opening to match the other seams. Press. With matching thread, topstitch around all sides of the apron, stitching close to the outside edges.

16. Turn under the raw edge of the waist straps ½˝, and topstitch to secure the hem. Go bake some cookies!

No Time 2 Pout—
Get That Quilt Out!

Dear Journal,

When I was a younger kid, I used 2 get straight A's. It seems 2 me that it was a lot easier then. Now that I am in 8th grade, I miss the mark by always getting a B or maybe 2 B's on my report card. I have 4 grading periods and 4 chances 2 get straight A's. Well, this semester I rec'd only 1 B+ in math! U would think that Mom & Dad would get me that go-cart they promised if I rec'd straight A's! The deal is simple: They say, straight A's or no go-cart! I'm pretty mad & I have 2 start all over next grading period cuz of that one B+! Rather than sit in my room and stare @ the ceiling, I will get out the quilt I am working on and finish as much of it as I can cuz in the end my pouting is wasting precious time. Who knows? I might make a small quilt 4 my math teacher. It couldn't hurt…

gtg,

No-Go-Cart Sara

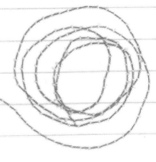

Sara's Hint

Attach a hand towel for messy projects. Cut a 5″ × 16″ rectangle from a hand towel. On each short edge (5″) cut the corners to make the ends pointed. Stitch around all sides of the towel with a zig-zag stitch to keep it from fraying. Fold the towel in half and press to crease the center. Position the folded towel, as desired, on the apron. Open the towel and stitch across the creased line. Refold the towel and topstitch along the fold line to secure in place.

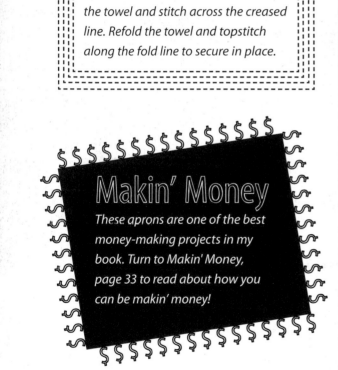

Makin' Money

These aprons are one of the best money-making projects in my book. Turn to Makin' Money, page 33 to read about how you can be makin' money!

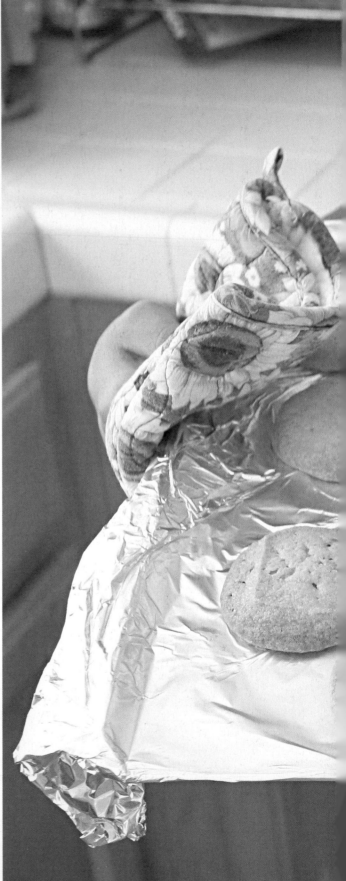

envelope
pillow

What a great place
to rest your head
after a long night
of cramming for
that biology quiz!

Finished Measurements:

16″ square

Materials

- ○ 16″ pillow form
- ○ 1¼ yards pretty fabric
- ○ Matching thread
- ○ Hand-sewing needle (optional)
- ○ Decorative buttons (optional)
- ○ Poly stuffing for Super Simple Stuffed Pillow, (see Super Simple Stuffed Pillow, page 68) (optional)

Instructions

1. Cut the fabric into the following sizes:

- ○ 1 square, 18″ × 18″, for pillow front
- ○ 2 rectangles, 18″ × 23″, for pillow back flaps

Sara's Hint

Pillow forms come in all sorts of sizes. It's easy to make different-sized envelope pillows—just do a little math:

Front, cut 1: *Add 2″ to each measurement of the pillow form. For a 12″ × 16″ pillow form, cut a 14″ × 18″ pillow front.*

Back flaps, cut 2: *Add 2″ to the width of the pillow form and 7″ to the length. For a pillow form 12″ × 16″, cut each back flap 14″ × 23″.*

2. Fold the pillow back flaps in half along the length (long side) of the flaps, wrong sides together. Press.

Fold the rectangles in half.

3. Place the pillow front fabric right side up on your work surface.

4. Position a back flap on the pillow front, lining up the outside raw edges. The folded edge will lie slightly over the center of the pillow front.

5. Lay the other folded back flap onto the front fabric, lining up the raw edges on the opposite side of the pillow. The folded edge of this flap will overlap the first flap by about 2½″. Pin all around.

6. Sew a ¼″ seam around all 4 sides of the pillow cover. Trim the corners by cutting them with scissors at an angle. Be careful not to cut through the stitching. Turn the pillow cover right side out, and press, making sure the seams are open.

7. Insert the pillow form through the back flaps. Use extra batting or cotton balls to fill in all 4 corners.

8. If you want, hand sew buttons along the outside of the envelope for a decorative touch.

It's time to lay your head down and take a nap on your new pillow!

The back flaps will overlap to create the envelope.

Cha-Ching

Dear Journal,

Great news! I finished 1 of the quilts I was making 4 my customer. (Yes, I have customers!) The business is going great! Mr. Henry just bought a new house and he wanted me 2 make a quilt 2 hang in the 2-story blank space on his new wall. He gave my mom the money and she brought it home 2 me today. It took me 8 weeks but now I am done. With the money I made I can buy some gr8 new clothes & tennis shoes! I might buy some video games instead. Bottom line is I feel fantastic!

$igned,

$ara

Super Simple Stuffed Pillow

Cut 2 squares of fabric 14½″ × 14½″ (or any other size you want). Place the squares right sides together, line them up, and pin the edges. Sew around the square ¼″ from the edge, leaving a 3″ opening. Trim the corners at an angle and turn the pillow right side out. Stuff with poly stuffing and hand stitch the opening closed. Make several and then have a pillow fight!

pj bottoms
(for boys or girls)

This is a really fun project to do with two or three friends at a sleepover! This is also a great birthday party idea. Here in California, my friends and I sometimes wear lightweight, non-see-through-fabric PJs outside. If you live in a colder climate, use some pretty flannels.

Materials

- PJ bottoms (make your own from a pattern, or use store-bought PJs or scrub pants)
- ¾ yard coordinating fabric for cuffs and waistband
- 1 package ½" elastic
- Matching thread
- Cloth measuring tape
- 2 large safety pins
- Hand-sewing needle

Makin' Money

The PJs can be cut out ahead of time for a PJ party. That way, you can host a party for boys or girls and advertise it as a "Make your own PJs to take home and keep" party.

Make Your Own PJs from a Pattern

I like to make my own PJs from a pattern, but you can use store-bought PJs or scrub pants too. If you're using store-bought bottoms, skip these instructions and go straight to PJ Cuffs on page 72. Here are some special tips if you are making your own PJ bottoms from a pattern.

○ Read page 28 for information about using a commercial pattern.

○ Read the pattern to find out how much fabric you need.

○ Follow the pattern's directions to cut out the PJ pieces. If you have directional fabric (see Directional Fabric, page 29), pay attention when cutting out the pieces.

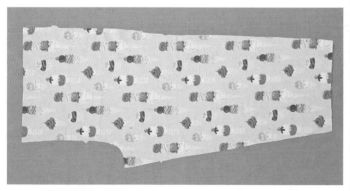

Cut out the pattern pieces.

○ Follow the pattern's directions to sew the parts of the PJs together, except do not finish the waistband or hem the legs.

Sew the PJs together.

Instructions

PJ CUFFS

1. Try on the pre-made PJ bottoms or scrubs. Measure and mark the hem length for your height, subtracting another 4″ for the cuff. Cut them shorter if you want capris. Trim the pant legs straight at the desired length.

2. Use a measuring tape to get the measurement around the leg opening (circumference). Add ½″ to this measurement to get the cutting length of the cuff. So, for example, if the leg opening is 15″ around, the cutting length would be 15½″.

Measure the leg opening.

3. Cut 2 rectangles of the coordinating fabric, 8½″ × the cuff's cutting length (PJ Cuffs, Step 2).

4. Join the ends of the cuff by sewing the short edges (8½″), right sides together, with a ¼″ seam. Press the seams open.

5. Fold each cuff in half around the length, wrong sides together, lining up the raw edges. Press.

6. For each leg, line up the raw edges of the cuff with the raw edge of the PJ leg opening, right sides together. Pin the cuff in place.

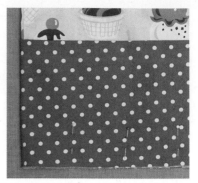

Pin the raw edges of the cuff to the leg opening.

7. Sew each cuff to a PJ leg, using a ¼″ seam. Press the seam toward the PJ leg.

PJ WAISTBAND

1. Cut off the PJ waistband. If you're using store-bought PJs or scrub bottoms, carefully cut off the waistband following the seam. If you're using a pattern, cut off only the amount the pattern says to turn under to make the waistband.

2. Measure around the waistband, as you did the leg opening. Add ½″ to this measurement to get the cutting length of the waistband.

3. Cut the coordinating fabric 7″ × the waistband's cutting length (PJ Waistband, Step 2).

4. Join the ends of the waistband to form a tube by sewing the short edges (7″), right sides together, with a ¼″ seam. Press the seam open.

5. Fold the waistband in half lengthwise and press to make a crease. Unfold the waistband and line up an edge with the edge of the PJ waist, right sides together. Pin, then sew the layers together with a ¼″ seam.

The waistband is sewn to the PJ waist.

6. Refold the waistband along the crease, line up the raw edges, and pin in place. Sew around the waistband ¼″ from the edge, stopping about 3″ from where you started, to leave an opening. Press the seam toward the PJ bottoms.

7. Wrap the elastic around your waist, without stretching it, so that fits snugly but comfortably. Cut it to that length.

8. With a safety pin, securely pin 1 end of the elastic to the inside of the waistband at the opening. Attach another safety pin to the other end of the elastic.

9. Use the attached safety pin to guide the loose end of the elastic through the waistband casing. The 2 ends of the elastic will meet at the opening.

10. Overlap the ends of the elastic by about ½″ and secure them with a safety pin. Use a zigzag stitch to sew the ends together.

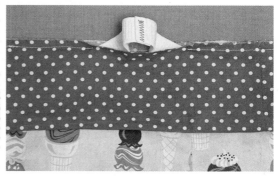

Sew the ends of the elastic together.

Sara's Hint

Before you sew the elastic together, make sure it isn't twisted in the waistband casing.

11. Hand sew the waistband's opening closed and you are done!

Show off you new jams at a sleepover party!

Dog Problems

Dear Journal,

Maddie and Cheetah R my 2 small dogs. Maddie is a Yorkie/Pomeranian mix & Cheetah is a Chihuahua mix. The problem is that Cheetah is well trained & never pees in the house while Maddie always pees
in the house, & you never know when! My mom has threatened 2 get rid of Maddie because of her wetting the floor. I got Maddie when I was in the 6th grade & I managed 2 get straight A's. I told Mom that Maddie is like my daughter, my only child! When I sew in my room, I put Maddie in a small basket with a towel & let her stay w/me. If I leave her on the floor—well, u know. Anyway, I put Maddie (who weighs 5 lbs) high on my shelf in the basket so she can watch me sew. She doesn't cry or wet the towel, but if I let her loose for any length of time she will sometimes wet the floor. I have to protect little Maddie because my mom has been dealing w/ this for 2 years & she says she is getting tired of Maddie. This is a great way 2 keep Maddie from wetting. She never wets her towel in the small basket; she just watches me sew & seems very content!

Signed,

Sara the Dog Whisperer

scrunchy

Scrunchies can be made to match any outfit. They make great gifts for your "sistahs." And, they are a great way to use fabric scraps from other projects.

Materials

- Scrap fabric, 1 rectangle 7″ × 14″
- 6½″ piece ¾″ elastic
- Matching thread
- 2 large safety pins

Instructions

Sara's Hint

Be sure to use only really beautiful fabrics that match many different colors of clothing. No one wants a plain, boring scrunchy! Try using the same fabric as the pillow or other projects and use all your scraps!

1. Press each of the short (7″) sides of the fabric rectangle under ½″.

2. Fold the fabric rectangle in half lengthwise (along the 14″ side), wrong sides together. Press to form a crease.

3. Unfold the fabric. Then fold in each side to the center crease, wrong sides together, as if you were making a strap (see Making Straps, pages 30–32). Press the folds.

Fold the sides in to the center crease.

4. Secure 1 end of the elastic to 1 end of the folded fabric with a safety pin.

Secure the elastic to the fabric.

5. Attach another safety pin to the loose end of the elastic, and place it outside the fabric. Refold the fabric at the crease. Topstitch ¼″ along the long, open side.

Topstitch along the long, open side.

6. Use the safety pin to guide the loose end of the elastic through the fabric casing, making sure not to twist the elastic.

7. Overlap the 2 ends of the elastic about ½″, making a circle, and stitch to secure them in place.

Stitch the elastic ends together.

8. Bring the edges of the casing together and stitch them closed.

You are done! Now, repeat this 50 more times and go make some money!!!

When You Can't Go, It's Time to Sew!

Dear Journal,

It's Friday & all the kids @ school R going 2 the roller rink & Mom & Dad say I can't go! They said that it's 2 late in the evening 4 me & that the rink has been attracting some tough characters lately. Well, I got angry & yelled (a little bit). Now, thanks 2 my big mouth, I am grounded! Because of my sewing machine & a couple of unfinished projects, I'll be just fine in my room, thank-you-very-much!

Signed,

Big Mouth Sara

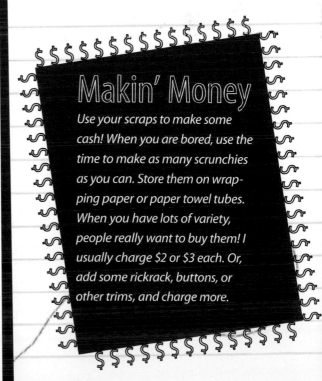

Makin' Money

Use your scraps to make some cash! When you are bored, use the time to make as many scrunchies as you can. Store them on wrapping paper or paper towel tubes. When you have lots of variety, people really want to buy them! I usually charge $2 or $3 each. Or, add some rickrack, buttons, or other trims, and charge more.

drawstring
bag

Drawstring bags make great gifts for friends and can be made to coordinate with all your outfits.

Finished Measurements:
17″ wide × 16″ tall

Materials

- ¾ yard theme fabric
- ⅜ yard coordinating fabric
- Matching thread
- Masking tape
- Pencil
- Large safety pin

Instructions

1. Cut the fabric into the following sizes:

From theme fabric, cut:

- 2 rectangles, 12½″ × 17½″, for body

- 2 strips, 4″ × width of fabric, for straps

From coordinating fabric, cut:

- 2 rectangles, 4″ × 18½″, for drawstring casing

- 2 rectangles, 4½″ × 17½″, for bottom

2. Pin a bottom rectangle to the long (17½″) bottom edge of a body rectangle, right sides together. Sew the pieces together using a ¼″ seam. Press toward the bottom. Repeat for the other bottom and body pieces.

3. Center and pin a casing rectangle to the top edge of a body rectangle, right sides together. The casing will hang over ½″ on each side of the body piece. Sew the pieces using a ¼″ seam. Press toward the casing. Repeat for the other casing.

Sara's Hint

The casing and bottom of this bag are close in size. Use masking tape and a pencil to label the pieces when you cut them, and the bag will go together super fast.

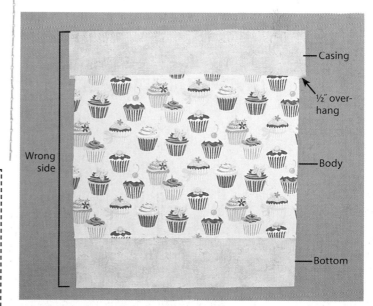

Sew the casing and bottom to the bag body.

4. Hem the short overhanging casing ends by folding them under about ½″. Topstitch the folds to keep them in place.

5. Fold the long raw edge of the casing under ¼″. Press to make a hem. Fold each casing piece in half lengthwise, toward the wrong side of the fabric, covering the seam where the casing was sewn to the body. Press.

6. Topstitch along each casing's hemmed edge to make a tube for the drawstring.

Sew the casing to make a drawstring tube.

Sara's Hint

I like to put pockets on these bags. Make a pocket by sewing a hemmed scrap of fabric (any size) to the body rectangle before assembling the bag. Adding pockets inside or outside the bag makes it even more useful.

7. Stack the 2 stitched body panels right sides together, line up the raw edges, seams, and tops of the folded casings. Pin in place.

8. Starting at the bottom hemmed edge of the casing, backstitch, then sew a ¼″ seam along the edge, down one side, across the bottom, and up the next side (see Turning Corners, page 24). On the last side, stop sewing and backstitch when you reach the bottom edge of the casing. Be careful not to sew through the casing tubes.

Leave the casings open when sewing the seams.

9. Fold the bottom corners, matching the side and bottom seams, to form a triangle. Pin in place. Measure and mark a line 2″ in from the triangle's point.

Mark a line 2″ from the folded point.

10. Sew along the marked line at each corner, backstitching at each end, then trim the seam allowance to ¼″. Turn the bag right side out, and see the nice square bottom you just made.

11. Use the 4″-wide theme fabric strips to make 2 straps, following the instructions in Making Straps, pages 30–32.

12. Secure a safety pin to 1 end of each strap. Use the safety pin to guide the straps through the casing tube. Tie the ends together.

You're ready to roll. These bags are perfect favors for pajama or birthday parties!

Inch by Inch It's a Cinch

Dear Journal,

I have signed up for another adult quilt class. This class is great but the quilt blocks R complicated & take a lot of time. Usually, Mom doesn't have 2 bug me 2 complete my quilt blocks but this time, my "eyes were 2 big for my fingers." Mom said that if I don't finish the blocks in time 4 the classes she has paid 4, that I will have 2 pay 4 the next class out of my own money. Anyway, I will be getting busy here in a few minutes!

Signed,

Feelin' Lazy Sara

Makin' Money

You can package a drawstring bag with a pair of PJs, a matching pillow, and a scrunchy by using the same fabrics. Just imagine—you now have a coordinated set of handmade items that you can sell to family and friends!

tote bag

Tote bags are all the rage and easy to make. Embellishments like patches, pins, funky buttons, or bling can turn yours into something awesome!

Finished Measurements:
approximately 15″ wide × 15″ tall

Materials

- ○ ½ yard Fabric A
- ○ ¼ yard Fabric B
- ○ ¼ yard Fabric C
- ○ ½ yard lining fabric
- ○ ⅜ yard strap fabric

- ○ Fusible interfacing or batting, 15½″ × 34½″
- ○ Matching thread
- ○ Parchment paper or appliqué pressing sheet

Instructions

1. Cut the fabric into the following sizes:

- ○ **Fabric A:** 2 rectangles, 12½″ × 15½″, for main body
- ○ **Fabric B:** 2 strips, 2½″ × 15½″, for middle strip
- ○ **Fabric C:** 2 strips, 3½″ × 15½″, for top strip
- ○ **Lining:** 1 rectangle, 15½″ × 34½″
- ○ **Straps:** 2 strips, 5″ × width of fabric

2. Using a ¼″ seam allowance, sew each middle strip to a top strip along the long edge (15½″), right sides together. Press the seams open.

3. Line up a long edge (15½″) of each main body rectangle with a middle strip from the sewn sets from Step 2, right sides together. Pin and sew the pieces together. Press the seams open.

Sew a strip set to each main body piece.

Sara's Hint

Whoops! Did you confuse the middle strip for the top strip when sewing the pieces together? Don't worry. Because the fabrics coordinate, it really doesn't matter in which order you sew the coordinating strips.

4. Layer the 2 pieced panels, right sides together. Sew the panels together along the bottom edges of the main body rectangles. Press the seams open.

Sew the bottom edges together.

5. Protect your ironing surface with parchment paper or an appliqué pressing sheet. Place the pieced body panel *wrong* side up on the protected surface. Line up the fusible (shiny) side of the interfacing or batting with the wrong side of the body. Fuse the interfacing or batting, following the manufacturer's directions.

Fuse the interfacing to the wrong side of pieced body.

6. Layer the body and lining, *wrong* sides together, and line up the edges. The interfacing or batting will be sandwiched between the 2 fabric layers. Using a long basting stitch, sew around all the edges, ¼˝ from the edge.

If necessary, trim the edges even with the edges of the pieced body.

7. Fold the sandwiched layers together along the bottom seam, lining side out. Pin the sides together, making sure the side seams are lined up. Sew each side seam with a ¼˝ seam allowance.

8. Fold the bottom corners, matching the side and bottom seams, to form a triangle. Pin in place. Measure and mark a line 2˝ in from the triangle's point.

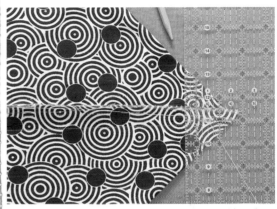

Fold the bottom corners to make a triangle.

9. Sew along the marked line at each corner, backstitching at each end, then trim the seam allowance to ¼˝. Turn the bag right side out, and see the nice square bottom you just made.

10. At the top opening of the tote, fold under ¼˝ of the edge toward the lining side. Press in place. Then turn under another ½˝ to make a hem. Press in place.

11. Use the strap fabric to make 2 straps, following the instructions in Making Straps, pages 30–32. I usually make my straps 30˝ long, but they can be as long or as short as you'd like.

12. Tuck the ends of each strap underneath the folded hem, 3″ in from each side seam. The straps will be facing down into the bag. Pin in place.

13. Sew around the entire opening, ¼″ from the bottom of the folded hem, remembering to backstitch when you start and stop sewing.

14. Fold the straps up and out of the bag, and pin in place. Secure the straps to the opening by sewing them ¼″ from the top edge of the bag. Backstitch to lock the stitches. Securing the straps reinforces them so the bag can carry more.

15. Press the tote and you are done!

Grab Mom and go shopping!

Don't Be a Copy Cat!

Dear Journal,

Good news! It's time 4 the science fair & I can use my sewing machine 2 recycle juice pouch containers & sew them into tote bags & purses. I found this idea on the Internet. Hey, it saves trees & energy! Great! I know it will be a unique project! My friend may do it 2, but she goes 2 a different school! Cool!

Signed,

Sara the Green

Makin' Money

These tote bags take some time to make, but they sell very well. Make a sample book to display the fabrics you offer. From your stash of large fabric pieces, cut small squares of each fabric option and glue them into a notebook. Keep your notebook with you at all times! When you are around family and friends, ask them if they like any of the samples, and then go home and make them tote bags from the fabric they've selected! The orders WILL COME!

rip-n-strip top

Who doesn't like to wear new clothes? With some basic sewing skills, you can whip up your own fab looks in a short time! This top has pretty ties in the back to keep things together.

Materials

For your fabric selection, use good-quality quilting cotton with a tight weave. Other fabrics won't tear as neatly. Yardage is based on 44"-wide unwashed fabric. Sizes are based on bust measurements: small = 21" or smaller, medium = 22"–30", and large = 30"–36".

Cotton theme fabric, for bodice and straps:

O Small: ¾ yard

O Medium: 1½ yards

O Large: 1¾ yards

2 coordinating cotton fabrics, for skirt:

O Small/medium: ½ yard each coordinating fabric

O Large: ¾ yard each coordinating fabric

O Matching thread

O Pencil or chopstick

O Chalk pencil

O Spray starch

O Hem decorations (optional): 1 roll 8"-wide tulle and silk flower petals

Instructions

MAKE THE BODICE

1. Fold the theme fabric in half lengthwise. Using the fabric like a towel, wrap it snugly around your bust and under your arms. Mark where the end meets the fabric, and add another 22" to that measurement. This is the bodice cutting length.

2. Decide how wide you need the bodice, from top to bottom, so that it covers your chest. Add another 1" to this number to get the bodice cutting width.

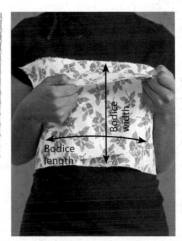

Measure your bodice length and width.

3. Use the bodice cutting length and width (Steps 1 and 2) to cut 2 identical rectangles from the theme fabric. For the small size, cut along the width of the fabric (selvage to selvage). For the medium and large sizes, cut the bodice pieces along the length of the fabric.

4. Fold the bodice rectangles in half widthwise (along the short side), wrong sides together. Stack the 2 pieces, lining up all the folded and cut edges, so you now have 4 layers. Then fold all 4 layers in half again, along the length, lining up all the cut edges. Pin the layers in place.

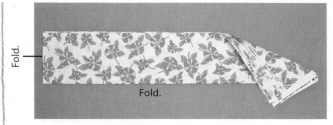

You now have 8 layers of fabric.

5. Measure in 10″ from the unfolded end of the stacked fabric. Make a mark with a chalk pencil on the long cut edge. Then measure in 6″ from the edge, and make another mark. Starting at the 6″ mark, draw a line 2″ down from the long cut edge. Use a ruler to connect the end of the line to the 10″ mark, creating an angle.

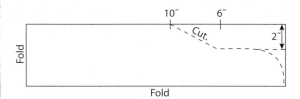

Mark cutting lines on the bodice.

6. Cut along the drawn lines with sharp fabric scissors, curving the corners at the narrow end. Be careful—you're cutting through all 8 layers of fabric. When you unfold the layers, you'll have 2 bodice pieces.

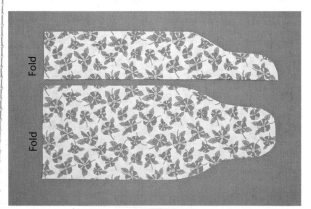

Cutting along the line will create the bodice ties.

Sewin' Sistah Sara

Dear Journal,

The book is coming along fine! The projects R fun & so easy! I hope all the kids that read the book & work on the projects will email me & tell me how they like it! I hope they tell me the good, the bad & the ugly! My plan is 2 create a group of "Sewin' Sistahs" across the country. That way we can keep each other up-2-date on what's happening!

Sewin' Sistah Sara

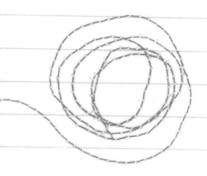

7. Completely unfold the bodice pieces and layer them, right sides together, lining up all the edges. Sew all around the bodice, ¼″ from the edge. Stop sewing about 3″ from where you started, to leave an opening.

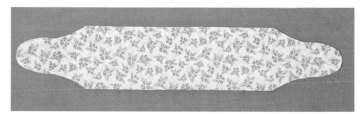

Line up the pieces and sew the layers together.

8. Turn the bodice right side out at the opening. With your fingers, the eraser end of a pencil, or a chopstick, push out the corners, being careful not to push through the stitching.

9. Fold under the seam allowance of the opening to match the other seams. Press. With matching thread, topstitch ¼″ around all sides of the bodice. Press, and set aside.

Topstitch around all sides of the bodice.

MAKE THE SKIRT

1. Fold each coordinating fabric piece in half lengthwise, so that it is 22″ wide. Press and cut the fabric along the fold to make 2 pieces from each length of fabric.

2. With your fabric scissors, take a snip about ½″ deep every 1″ to 3″ along the selvage edge of the fabric. The snips will help you easily tear strips from the cotton. No kidding! You actually get to tear up your fabric!

3. Grab the fabric firmly at a snip, and carefully tear strips from the fabric. The strips will be different widths, and the amount you need depends on how big you want your top to be. For my top, I used 26 strips, 13 from each coordinating fabric. Start with a few strips; you can always rip more if you need to. Press every strip with spray starch, to make it easier to sew.

Sara's Hint

If your fabric shreds when you rip it, or it doesn't rip straight, the problem is probably the fabric you're using. Be sure to use a good-quality cotton fabric—not rayon, a looser-weave fabric, or a polyester blend. To ensure that the cotton fabric is the best you can get, look for quilter's cottons at quilt shops.

4. Sew the torn strips together with a ¼″ seam, alternating strips from one coordinating fabric to the other to form stripes. You're creating a whole new striped fabric. Clip off all the loose threads and press all the seams to one side.

Join the strips to make striped fabric.

5. Keep sewing the strips together until the striped fabric measures the same as the bodice cutting length (Make the Bodice, Step 1, page 89). If you don't have enough strips, rip some more, press them, and keep sewing.

6. Pin and sew the 2 end strips of the striped fabric together to form a tube.

7. Fold the striped tube in half widthwise, and trim 1 edge straight with a rotary cutter or scissors.

Trim the edge straight.

8. Use a long basting stitch and sew ¼″ from the top trimmed edge. Tie a knot at 1 end of the loose thread tails, then gently pull the other end to gather small pleats into the skirt.

FINISH THE TOP

1. Line up the gathered edge of the skirt with the long straight bottom edge of the bodice, right sides together. Pin the layers using lots of pins to keep the gathers in place.

2. Sew a straight seam ¼˝ along the straight edge of the bodice. Press the seam toward the bodice. Add an optional topstitch along the seam to secure the bodice fold.

A pretty tie in the back keeps things together. The ties are those funky ends on the bodice that you sewed. Just make a knot to close your top!

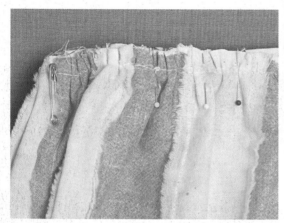

Pin and sew the bodice to the skirt.

5. Sew the straps in place ¼˝ from the top of the bodice. Trim off excess strap. If necessary, trim excess fabric from the hemline. Sew the hem.

Now go dancin'!

3. Cut a strip of theme fabric, 8˝ by the width of the fabric, and, following the instructions on pages 30–32, make 1 long strap. Cut the finished strap in half to make 2 straps.

4. Try on the top. Position the straps on the bodice so they are comfortable and cover your bra straps. Pin them in place. Fold under and pin the hemline to the desired length.

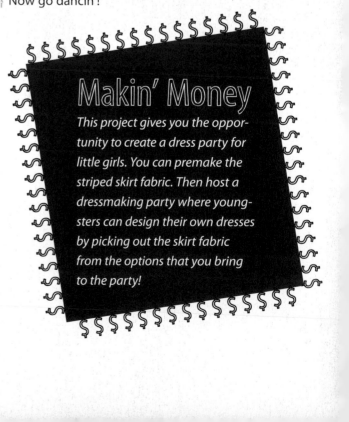

Makin' Money

This project gives you the opportunity to create a dress party for little girls. You can premake the striped skirt fabric. Then host a dressmaking party where youngsters can design their own dresses by picking out the skirt fabric from the options that you bring to the party!

Optional Hem Embellishment

As an option, I took a roll of 8″-wide tulle ribbon and cut a piece long enough to fit around the hem. Then I folded it lengthwise to create a 2-layer 4″-wide ribbon. I sewed the open edges of the ribbon to the hemline, leaving an opening about 5″ wide. Then I gently stuffed the tulle casing with washable designer silk petals (see Resources, page 111). I spread them throughout the casing and sewed the opening closed. Voilà! I have an even cooler-looking top!

Tulle hem with silk petals

school
folder

No more plain, boring folders for you. Now you can style your way through English class with a custom-made folder.

Materials

- 1 yard heavyweight double-sided fusible interfacing (See Sara's Hint below.)
- ½ yard main fabric
- ½ yard coordinating fabric, for lining and accents
- Matching thread
- Pen, pencil, or permanent marker
- Chalk pencil
- Parchment paper or appliqué pressing sheet
- 2″ pieces of 1½″-wide iron-on hook-and-loop tape, or 1 nickel-sized (or larger) iron-on hook-and-loop tape dot

Sara's Hint

I use fast2fuse® for this project. It comes in regular and heavyweight versions and is 28″ wide from the bolt, so 1 yard is enough for 2 folders. The fusible adhesive is on both sides of the interfacing, making this a no-fuss project. It can be found in most quilt stores and some fabric stores. Use the regular weight for this project.

Instructions

1. Cut the interfacing into a 12½″ × 32½″ rectangle. You can use your rotary mat and ruler to do this. Or draw the lines on the interfacing with a pen or marker and carefully cut the rectangle with a pair of sharp scissors.

2. Place the rectangle flat and lengthwise in front of you. At the lower right-hand corner, measure up 4″ on the short side edge, and make a mark there.

3. At the upper right-hand corner, measure in 9″ along the top long edge, and make a mark.

4. Draw a diagonal line between the 2 marks. Carefully cut on the line and remove that corner. This will be the pocket for your folder. *Important:* Before you move the interfacing, write the word "inside" on the side facing you. Then flip it over and write "outside" on the other side.

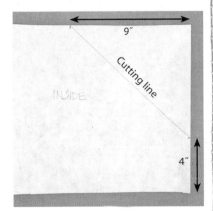

Mark the cutting lines.

Sara's Hint

Take the interfacing totally off the table when you're not using it, so you don't accidentally cut off a piece.

Sara's Hint

It took me several tries to finally get this project made beautifully. Be patient. The more you make this folder, the better you will become at it! Don't get discouraged by the difficult parts. Just do your best and don't quit!

5. Lay the lining fabric smooth and flat, lengthwise on your work surface, right side down. Place the interfacing on top of the fabric, with the outside facing up. With scissors, trim the fabric about 6″ from the short straight edge of the interfacing. On the remaining 3 sides, trim the fabric at least 1″ away from the interfacing.

Trim the lining fabric.

6. Place parchment paper or an appliqué pressing sheet on your ironing surface. Lay the interfacing on the protected surface with the inside facing up. Then position the trimmed lining fabric, right side up, on top of the interfacing, making sure the fabric has at least 1″ overhang on 3 sides.

7. Following the manufacturer's directions, iron the lining fabric to the interfacing. You are ironing the fabric to the folder's inside. If you're using fast2fuse®, it likes a lot of steam. Not all brands do, though, so make sure you read the directions.

8. When the fabric is fused to the inside, flip the interfacing over (the outside is now facing up). Fold the fabric edges over the edges of the interfacing, and carefully iron them in place. You want to make sure that the corners are nicely tucked over the edge. We'll sew them down later, so don't worry if they open some.

Sara's Hint

BE CAREFUL! Make sure you touch the iron to the fabric only, not to the exposed interfacing. The interfacing's adhesive will melt on your iron if you touch it directly. Ask an adult to help you. Be careful so you don't burn your fingers!

Don't let the hot iron touch the exposed interfacing.

9. Lay the main fabric smooth and flat, lengthwise on your work surface, right side up. Lay the interfacing, with the outside facing up, on top of the fabric. Hold the interfacing down to keep it flat, then trace around all the edges with a chalk pencil, marking the right side of the main fabric. Remove the interfacing.

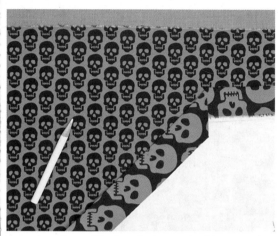

Trace the edges of the interfacing on the fabric.

10. Using a ruler, draw a straight line 3″ in from the traced line along the short straight edge. Carefully cut the fabric straight along this line. Then cut around the remaining traced lines, adding a ½″ allowance to the outer edge of the line.

11. Fold the short straight edge under 1″ toward the wrong side of the fabric. Press. Fold and press the other 3 edges along the drawn line, folding them under about ½″ to the wrong side of the fabric.

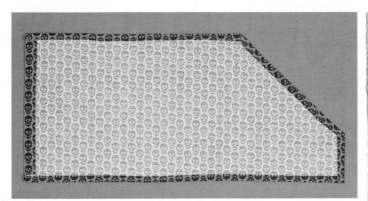

The short straight edge is folded under 1˝.

12. Place the outside of the interfacing facing up, lengthwise on the ironing surface. Carefully position the trimmed and pressed main fabric on top, right side up. Three of the edges (top, bottom, and angled edge) will match the interfacing's edges exactly. The fourth edge (the short straight edge) will show the 6˝ overlap of the lining fabric. It's supposed to be this way. Fuse the positioned fabric to the interfacing. Don't worry if the edges don't stay down; just make sure the fabric is fused well in the center.

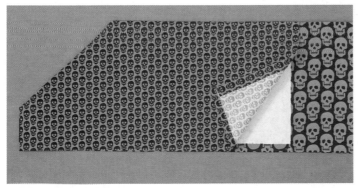

Position the main fabric.

13. Sew around the fabric-covered interfacing ¼˝ from the edge. Then sew around the interfacing again, this time stitching ½˝ from the edge.

Stitch along the edge twice to secure the fabric.

14. Sew 2 lines ¼˝ apart along the edge of the main fabric where it overlaps the lining fabric. The fabric is now secured to the interfacing.

15. Use a spiral notebook as a guide to fold the interfacing. Fold the angled edge in toward the lining to create a pocket with enough room to hold the notebook (see photo on page 104). Pin the pocket flap in place, then stitch down the pocket's short side and bottom edge.

No Invitation?
Time for Your Own
Creation!

Dear Journal,

My friend from my old school didn't get invited 2 a sleepover party b/c her mom doesn't know the other girl's mom. She was pretty bummed. I told her 2 come over & we would sew a super-cute blouse that would make all the girls beg 2 know where she bought it from. Then she could say it's an original design! G2G. She is at the door & we've got work 2 do.

Signed,

Party 4 Sara 2

Makin' Money

These folders REALLY SELL! Personalize your folders with embroidered names. Use an embroidery machine if you have one, or ask the ladies at the sewing machine store to embroider for you. Embroider the name on the folder fabric without worrying about placement. Just put the name somewhere on the front and it will look great!

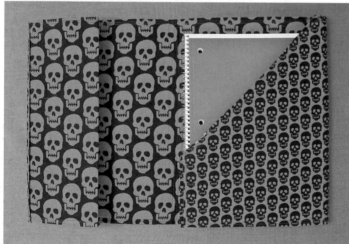

Use a spiral notebook for accurate folding.

16. Fold the folder completely closed. The overlap becomes the folder's flap. Crease the folder where it needs to fold.

Sara's Hint

If you're having trouble making your interfacing fold, sew a straight line where you want the fold line. You can even sew the line a couple of times, if needed. This makes the interfacing crease and fold more easily.

17. Position the iron-on hook-and-loop tape so that 1 piece is on the inside of the flap and the other piece is on the outside of the folder. Iron the tape following the manufacturer's directions.

Done! Take it to school and take orders for more! Make that money, Honey!

the ✓-lists

Okay, so you've got projects to make and parties to throw.

But what about some of the basics of setting yourself up in business?

On the following pages, I wanted to give you some ideas to grow your business beyond your bedroom. From selling at fairs to getting business cards, there are so many little and big ways you can stretch your reach!

9. Provide one sample of each of your products you're selling as a demo model. For instance, if you're making MP3 covers, have on a stand with an MP3 player in it so customers can play with the covers and see how it works. If you can, keep the other ones wrapped or bagged. Otherwise, they will mess with all of them and you risk your products getting dirty or breaking.

10. Absolutely, positively keep a small basket or jar of candy on the table. Kisses, M&Ms and other small nibbles make people feel welcome and also cause children to drag their parents to your table.

11. Keep all of these supplies in a large tote box so you're ready to go to set up at a moment's home from a sale,

tive and make customers feel welcome. But don't borrow your mother's antique crystal to set up at the table! Things break easily in the packing.

4. Do provide a cup with pens. People take notes and they write checks. The pens are another friendly way to welcome your customers to your booth. You can even decorate the pens with silk flowers or do-dads to make them more fun.

5. Absolutely provide business cards and any promotional fliers with the information about what other products and services you offer. It's one thing to be able to sell five scrunchies to a customer. It's a whole lot better if that customer then hires you to throw a party for her 10-year-

will mess with all of them and y ucts getting dirty or breaking.

10. Absolutely, positively keep a s of candy on the table. Kisses, N small nibbles make people fee also cause children to drag the your table.

11. Keep all of these supplies in a la so you're ready to go to set up notice. When you come home fr make a list of what you need t box, both your products and y Make sure the box has your na phone number written with a

6. Have a receipt book on hand to writ your sales. You can get a receipt boo of dollars at any office supply or large write a receipt every time you sell so will be better able to keep track of yo

7. Make sure you have a cash box with r and some dollars to make change. Thi spending money! This is money you ke to run your business.

8. Keep a list of your inventory—what yo with you and, at the end of the day, wh coming home with.

9. Provide one sample of each of your pro you're selling as a demo model. For inst you're making MP3 covers, have on a sta an MP3 player in it so customers can play covers and see how it works. If you can, other ones wrapped or bagged. Otherw will mess with all of them and you risk yo ucts getting dirty or breaking.

10. Absolutely, positively keep a small baske of candy on the table. Kisses, M&Ms and small nibbles make people feel welcome also cause children to drag their parents your table.

11. Keep all of these supplies in a large tote b so you're ready to go to set up at a mome notice. When you come home from a sale make a list of what you need to refill ir box, both your products and your supl

{dress up your selling space}

Are you thinking about selling your crafts and projects at a church bazaar, craft fair or other place where people will be gathered? The booth or table you are selling from is like a mini-store. If it looks appealing to customers, it can help bring them in to look at your products. Here are some things you can do to "dress up" your selling space.

1. Have a pretty table cloth or some other cover to hide the surface areas. Folding tables are very useful, but not very pretty. A bright, cheerful tablecloth can attract customers to your table faster than anything else.

2. Make signs with information and pricing and frame the signs in pretty picture frames. For instance, if you have a basket of scrunchies for sale, put a small, framed sign with the price in front of the basket. Customers like to know how much something costs.

3. Make room on the table for one or two decorative items. A small lamp, a vase with flowers, a box with scrap paper—these things are attractive and make customers feel welcome. But don't borrow your mother's antique crystal to set up at the table! Things break easily in the packing.

4. Do provide a cup with pens. People take notes and they write checks. The pens are another friendly way to welcome your customers to your booth. You can even decorate the pens with silk flowers or do-dads to make them more fun.

5. Absolutely provide business cards and any promotional fliers with the information about what other products and services you offer. It's one thing to be able to sell five scrunchies to a customer. It's a whole lot better if that customer then hires you to throw a party for her 10-year-old daughter! Make sure you have plenty of cards and fliers because they will be taken. Have a stash under the table in case you run out.

6. Have a receipt book on hand to write receipts for your sales. You can get a receipt book for a couple of dollars at any office supply or large store. If you write a receipt every time you sell something, you will be better able to keep track of your business.

7. Make sure you have a cash box with rolls of coins and some dollars to make change. This is not your spending money! This is money you keep on hand to run your business.

8. Keep a list of your inventory—what you bring with you and, at the end of the day, what you're coming home with.

9. Provide one sample of each of your products you're selling as a demo model. For instance, if you're making MP3 covers, have on a stand with an MP3 player in it so customers can play with the covers and see how it works. If you can, keep the other ones wrapped or bagged. Otherwise, they will mess with all of them and you risk your products getting dirty or breaking.

10. Absolutely, positively keep a small basket or jar of candy on the table. Kisses, M&Ms and other small nibbles make people feel welcome and also cause children to drag their parents to your table.

11. Keep all of these supplies in a large tote box so you're ready to go to set up at a moment's notice. When you come home from a sale, make a list of what you need to refill in the box, both your products and your supplies. Make sure the box has your name and phone number written with a permanent pen on the outside and store it under your table at the event.

businesscards

With all of the programs on the market to design your own business cards and brochures/fliers, you can do this at home pretty easily. And if you can't, find one of your favorite computer geeks to help!

Ingredients for a business card are:

1. Your name.

2. Your business name, if you have one.

3. Your phone number(s).

4. Your address, in case they need to mail a contract to you or something!

5. Your email address.

6. Make sure you card is attractive and easy to read. Don't use a font smaller than 10 points.

7. Have someone else read the card before printing to make sure there are no typos or mistakes!

Sara Trail
sewsara@email.com

925.555.1234
1234 Sew Ave.
Antioch, CA 94444

sew
with
sara

Super-Cool Tote Bag

Hand-made from funky red, white and black fabric, this great bag can be used at the beach, at school or as a shopping tote.

To order, call or email Sara!
925.555.1234 ■ sewsara@email.com

flier

A flier or brochure provides the same information as the business card but gives a bigger picture of what you offer. Besides the information above, include:

1. Pictures of your products. Make sure the pictures are clear and well-lit.

2. Descriptions of your products and/or services.

3. Prices of your services or products. You might not want to put this in a flier in case you have to change something later on. It's your call.

4. When you're writing your descriptions you want to sell your products and services, but you don't want to exaggerate about them.

5. A brochure is usually folded. A flier is usually a single sheet. You can also write up several sheets of information, staple your business card to the upper corner, and be done with it. It's up to you. But always make sure to proof-read your work and that it looks neat.

party*planning*
checklist

first   last

CLIENT NAME

eMAIL ADDRESS

ADDRESS

PHONE NUMBER

EVENT DATE   PARTY THEME

EVENT TIME   # OF GUESTS

AGE/GENDER OF GUESTS

EVENT LOCATION

List items needed for the party.
Who will provide them, you or the host?

Food   ○ host   ○ you

Music   ○ host   ○ you

Games   ○ host   ○ you

Materials *(fabric, glue, paints)*   ○ host   ○ you

_____

_____

_____

_____

Special Equiptment *(electrical outlets,*   ○ host   ○ you
tables, or miscellaneous supplies)

_____

_____

_____

_____

Clean-Up Supplies   ○ host   ○ you

_____

_____

_____

_____

How much time will it take to complete the project? _____

Who will supervise?

_____

NAME

_____

PHONE NUMBER

Payment

○ per person _____

○ per hour _____

○ other _____

> Your mother was right: How you look and act when you're trying to build your business is important to getting customers.

Here are some tips on how to present yourself:

1. Make sure you're dressed neatly and that your clothes are clean and pressed. You can still dress like a teen, but be neat about it.

2. When you're speaking to your customers, be friendly and speak clearly. If you mumble or don't make eye-contact, they won't be comfortable with you and they need to be if they're going to hire you for other jobs.

3. Always, always be polite and watch your language. Not just the bad words, but also the "umms" and "likes" and "you knows." You want your customers to take you seriously and they won't do that if you sound too young.

4. Enjoy speaking to your customers. Ask how they are doing. If they bring children with them, talk to the kids. Maybe even have a small gift or piece of candy for them (Don't offer the candy without first checking with their mom though!) They are coming to you because they are interested in what you do. Even if they don't buy something, talk to them and thank them for coming. You never know when they'll come back or send someone else over to buy from you.

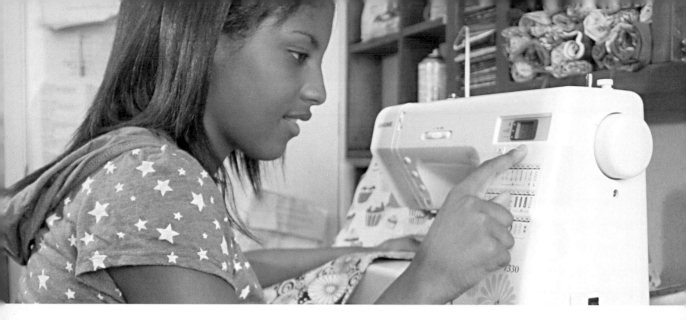

resources

Note: Fabrics used in the projects shown may not be currently available, as fabric manufacturers keep most fabrics in print for only a short time.

For many of the fabrics used in my projects:
Robert Kaufman Fabrics
www.robertkaufman.com

Michael Miller Fabrics
www.michaelmillerfabrics.com

For high-quality threads:
Sulky threads
www.sulky.com

For the silk flower petals used in the Rip–n-Strip Top:
Bella Nonna Quilts Co.
www.bellanonnaquilt.com

For fast2fuse fusible interfacing:
C&T Publishing
www.ctpub.com

For a list of other fine books from C&T Publishing, ask for a free catalog:
C&T Publishing, Inc.
P.O. Box 1456
Lafayette, CA 94549
(800) 284-1114
Email: ctinfo@ctpub.com
Website: www.ctpub.com

C&T Publishing's professional photography services are now available to the public. Visit us at www.ctmediaservices.com.

For quilting supplies:
Cotton Patch
1025 Brown Ave.
Lafayette, CA 94549
Store: (925) 284-1177
Mail order: (925) 283-7883
Email: CottonPa@aol.com
Website: www.quiltusa.com

Great Titles from
C&T Publishing

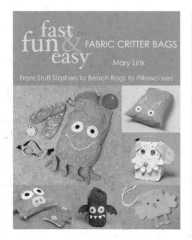

fast fun & easy FABRIC CRITTER BAGS
Mary Link
From Stuff Stashers to Beach Bags to Pillowcases

The Best of
Sewing Machine
Fun for Kids
POSSIBILITIES

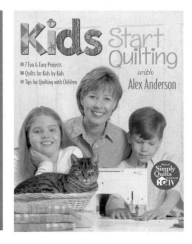

Kids Start Quilting
■ 7 Fun & Easy Projects
■ Quilts for Kids by Kids
■ Tips for Quilting with Children
with Alex Anderson
Best of Simply Quilts HGTV

miy make it your
sew hip
Easy Step-by-Step Instructions   Unmistakably You Projects   Includes Sewing 101 DVD
Shannon Mullen

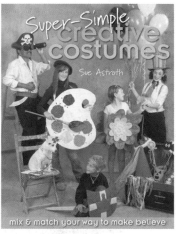

Super-Simple
creative costumes
Sue Astroth
mix & match your way to make believe

FUSING FUN!
Fast Fearless Art Quilts
LAURA WASILOWSKI